THE ENCHIRIDION
ON FAITH, HOPE AND LOVE

St. Augustine

THE ENCHIRIDION
ON FAITH, HOPE AND LOVE

Edited with an Introduction

by

HENRY PAOLUCCI

With an analysis and historical
appraisal by Adolph von Harnack

A GATEWAY EDITION

HENRY REGNERY COMPANY   CHICAGO

Manufactured in the United States of America, 11-61

CONTENTS

> . . . *the ideas of this man furnished the themes*
> *for the piety and theology of more than a thou-*
> *sand years. No one possessed the "whole"*
> *Augustine, but all lived upon the fragments of*
> *his spirit from which each appropriated and*
> *understood what was "adapted" to his own*
> *wants.*[1]

REINHOLD SEEBERG

INTRODUCTION

The *Enchiridion* on faith, hope, and love was written, St. Augustine tells us, to supply a summary of his thought on the essential teachings of the Christian religion. The Roman Laurentius to whom it was originally addressed in 421 A.D. (and about whom little else is known) had asked specifically for a handbook of "Augustinian" answers to questions which were apparently then troubling the minds of many Christians in cultured Roman society.[2] St. Augustine himself, in the opening paragraphs, stresses the importance of the questions posed to him; and it appears from his reassessment of the work in his severely self-critical *Retractions* that he was by no means dissatisfied with his handbook of answers, that, in fact, he considered it to be "a sufficiently thorough survey" of the true content of Christian wisdom.[3]

How well the *Enchiridion* may have served the needs of the "beloved Laurentius" for whom

---

[1] Reinhold Seeberg, *Text-book of the History of Doctrines,* trans. by Charles E. Hay (Philadelphia, 1905), Vol. I, p. 368.
[2] Pierre Batiffol, *Le Catholicisme de Saint Augustin* (4th ed., Paris, 1929), pp. 511-12.
[3] St. Augustine, *Retractationes,* 2.89(63), in J. P. Migne, *Patrologia Latina,* XXXII, col. 655.

it was written, we have no way of knowing. But surely the abundance of manuscripts, the prominence of citations from it in the *Sentences* of Peter Lombard, and the number of important scholastic treatises modelled upon it are a sufficient proof of its continuous and profound influence throughout the Middle Ages.[4] Renaissance humanists, Protestant reformers, theologians of the Counter-Reformation, rigorous Jansenists— all praised the work and drew upon it for doctrinal nourishment. For the Benedictines of St. Maur it was "verily a book of gold, to be kept in hand night and day."[5] J. Rivière, in the introduction to his elaborately annotated Latin-French edition of 1947, has fittingly remarked: "Of all the works of St. Augustine, no other one, surely, has occupied the attention of theologians more continuously than the *Enchiridion*. And today, judges the least partial are unanimous in acknowledging that it is entitled to such distinction."[6] Reviewing its reputation among modern scholars, he especially cites the praise of Tixeront, Portalié and Cayre, and reminds his readers of the detailed analyses of the work included in the doctrinal histories of Reinhold Seeberg and Adolph von Harnack.[7]

But while there is general agreement that St.

[4] See *Enchiridion*, text, translation and notes by Jean Rivière, in the Bibliothèque Augustinienne, Oeuvres de S. Augustin, première série: Opuscules, IX: *Exposés généraux de la foi* (Paris, 1947), pp. 91 and 95; see also Martin Grabman, *Die Geschichte Der Scholastischen Methode* (Berlin, 1957), Vol. I, pp. 134-35.

[5] Migne, *Patrologia Latina*, Vol. XL, "In sextum tomum praefatio," cols. 9-10.

[6] Rivière, *op. cit.*, p. 79.

[7] *Ibid.*, p. 87.

Augustine's *Enchiridion* supplies "a fairly complete compendium of his whole theology and the system on which it rests," [8] many scholars today find it difficult to justify the structure of the work. According to one recent editor, it is simply an "awkward" and "patently artificial schematism" by means of which St. Augustine "tries unsuccessfully to subdue his natural digressive manner." [9] Even Eugène Portalié, in his brilliant study for the *Dictionnaire de théologie catholique*, feels hard-pressed to account for the "division of theology—at first sight so strange—in the *Enchiridion*." [10] Seeberg, too, with all his admiration for the work, marvels at the skill with which the author manages to interweave "his profoundest ideas upon sin, grace and predestination" into such a scheme. What seems strange to some and awkward to others is, evidently, St. Augustine's procedure in reducing "all Christian doctrine to the three theological virtues," [11] the contents of which he expounds in terms of the Apostle's Creed, or Symbol, and the Lord's Prayer. It seems, at first sight, to be a kind of tour de force. And yet, not only in the *Enchiridion* but also in his treatise *On Christian Doctrine* we find St. Augustine insisting without reservation that there is no better way of summarizing the whole body of Christian teaching

[8] Louis A. Arand, *St. Augustine: Faith, Hope and Charity* (Westminster, Md., 1947), p. 6.
[9] *Augustine: Confessions and Enchiridion,* trans. and ed. by Albert C. Outler (Philadelphia, 1955), p. 20.
[10] Eugène Portalié, *A Guide to the Thought of St. Augustine,* trans. by Ralph J. Bastian (Chicago, 1960), p. 309.
[11] *Ibid.,* p. 309.

than by expounding thoroughly "the proper objects of faith, hope and love; for these must be the chief, nay, the exclusive objects of pursuit in religion." [12] And Harnack, surely one of the most learned students of doctrinal history, writes emphatically: "When we seek to determine what has been accomplished by an ancient Church theologian as a teacher of the Church, we must examine his expositions of the Symbol." [13]

But perhaps the best way to be disabused of the notion that the structure of the *Enchiridion* is unsystematic is to compare it with the structures used for the systematic exposition of philosophical knowledge by the greatest secular thinkers from Aristotle to Hegel. St. Augustine's teachers in philosophy, the Neoplatonists, were great systematizers; and one should not forget that he himself, before his conversion, had completed the intellectual ascent to the topmost rung of the Platonic *scala amoris*, where, "in the flash of one trembling glance," he saw, as he tells us in the *Confessions*, *Id Quod Est*, the divine principle of universal order, source of all Being, of all Truth, of all Goodness.[14] When he descended from that height of pagan wisdom to kneel at the foot of the Cross, he by no means forgot what he had seen there. Indeed, as Harnack observes, when that "fear of the Lord" which is the beginning of wisdom was awakened

[12] Saint Augustine, *On Christian Doctrine*, trans. and with an Introduction by D. W. Robertson, Jr. (New York, 1958), pp. 31-33; *Enchiridion*, Ch. 4.
[13] Adolph von Harnack, *History of Dogma*, trans. by James Millar (London, 1898), Vol. V, p. 95.
[14] *Confessions*, Bk. VII, Ch. XVII.

in him, St. Augustine did not abandon the systematic Neoplatonist tendency of thought which had enabled him to transcend the particularized "domains of objective secular knowledge"; on the contrary, he continued philosophically in the same direction, advancing far beyond his masters. Augustine, Harnack asserts,—

brought to an end the development of ancient philosophy by completing the process which led from the naive objective to the subjective objective. He found what had been long sought for: the making of the inner life the starting-point of reflection on the world. And he did not give himself up to empty dreams, but investigated with a truly "physiological psychology" all conditions of the inner life, from its elementary processes up to the sublimest moods; he became, because he was the counterpart of Aristotle, the true Aristotle of a new science.[15]

Harnack emphasizes in other parts of his work the historical importance of the parallel suggested here between Aristotle, the supreme philosopher of Nature, and St. Augustine, the supreme philosopher of Grace.[16] It is by no means a far-fetched comparison; St. Augustine himself, in the *Opus Imperfectum* (III, 199), reports that his great intellectual opponent, the Pelagian Julian of Eclanium, had given him, derisively, the title "Aristoteles Poenorum." But we have only to contrast the basic naturalistic principles of theoretic, practical and productive science distinguished by Aristotle[17] with the principles of Christian faith, hope and love, as defined by

---

[15] Harnack, *op. cit.*, Vol. V, p. 107.
[16] *Ibid.*, pp. 9, 11, and 107-109; Vol. VI, pp. 156-57.
[17] Aristotle, *The Nicomachean Ethics*, trans. by H. Rackham (Cambridge, 1947), pp. 324-73.

St. Augustine in the *Enchiridion* to appreciate at once the appropriateness of the comparison.

St. Augustine seems to have had, unfortunately, no direct acquaintance with any of the major works of Aristotle. Nevertheless, one finds in his writings a marvelously thorough account of the Aristotelian conception of Nature, in which all things, from the lowest to the highest, are moved to do what they do and to be what they are, by a single principle—an erotic gravitational force—itself unmoved, that moves all things as the object of their desires. It was, no doubt, from the writings of the Neoplatonists—who might not less fittingly be called neo-Aristotelians —that St. Augustine first learned of this Aristotelian conception. But apparently he soon made it his own, identifying its principle, *cupiditas*, the power of Eros, or Cupid, as the antithesis of Judaic *agape* or *caritas,* the wholehearted *amor Dei* that builds the heavenly city.

According to the Aristotelian conception,[18] the erotic principle that holds the universe of nature together moves man, through his will, to pursue happiness, and through his intellect, to pursue knowledge. These practical and theoretic activities are distinct at first. Yet, if carried forward intelligently, they tend to unite, the goals of happiness and truth fusing together to form a single end which is the ultimate good of man. Unfortunately, however, it is difficult to advance

---

[18] The exposition here summarizes the central arguments of Aristotle's *Nicomachean Ethics, Metaphysics,* and *Politics.*

to the point of unity; indeed, according to Aristotle, happiness and truth in their advanced forms are not even approximately attainable by men until they have accomplished all that is necessary to form a well-ordered political society, which must be large enough to supply all the material needs of its members, powerful enough to secure their persons and possessions against external enemies, and authoritative enough to maintain, with the consent of the governed, an internal system of laws supported by public education. Thus, in summing up the ethical and political experience of the Greek world, Aristotle distinguishes three basic principles: first, in the practical sphere, that all men by nature desire to be happy; second, in the theoretic sphere, that all men by nature desire to know; and third, in the productive sphere, that all men by nature desire to build up the life of fellowship in a well-ordered community. And, St. Augustine, as often as he undertakes to contrast Christian and pagan experience, makes use of precisely these Aristotelian principles—though the expressions he usually adopts are those of the popular moralists of Cicero's time who translated and vulgarized them for the Roman world.[19]

In his apologetic writings addressed to persons educated in the Platonic-Aristotelian tradition, St. Augustine attempts to make the Christian

[19] In Book XIX of the *City of God,* St. Augustine reviews the pagan schemes for the attainment of the *summum bonum* in accordance with the distinctions drawn by that "most learned of the Romans," M. Varro (116 B.C.–28 B.C.) in his *De Philosophia,* which has not come down to us.

message intelligible by saying, in effect: To some human beings who have grown weary and heavy laden while attempting to build up a community in which the natural desires to be happy and to know might attain a fair measure of satisfaction, Jesus Christ, God's grace in the world, comes saying, I am the way to that happiness, the truth of that knowledge, the very life of that community you seek. That is to say, when and if it is given, God's grace comes into the world to meet the needs of men as they present themselves in the so-called natural order, which is really the psychological disorder of fallen nature. For surely it is a mark of disorder that the desire for happiness should manifest itself in the growing child as it does, so inordinately, like the pull of wild horses, long before reason awakens to the pursuit of knowledge. But in the full life of grace, after immediate needs are met, the disorder is corrected: faith, with its knowledge, comes first, then the happiness of hope, and finally the everlasting community of love. Thus, according to St. Augustine, is the age-old problem of human conduct (which, as the ancients knew, consists in the disorderly, irrational inclination of the appetites and passions) rendered transparent for all by Christian doctrine; and thus, for those who abide in grace, is it ultimately resolved.

This contrast between the pagan principles of human conduct and the Christian virtues is most compactly and strikingly drawn by St. Augustine in the concluding paragraphs of the fourteenth book of the *City of God*, where he speaks of the two cities built by two contrary loves, the one man-centered, the other centered in God. There he explicitly contrasts the *amor sui* that builds great nations with the *amor Dei* that builds the Christian fellowship, the kind of knowledge in which worldly men take pride with the pious faith of the servants of God, and the good things of the body and of the mind which the wise of the world pursue with the restful hope of the faithful who look to heaven for their reward. But it is in the *Enchiridion*, where St. Augustine puts all polemic aside, that the contents of Christian faith, hope and love are displayed most meaningfully, and—despite what some critics have said to the contrary— with the kind of emphasis and proportion which systematic philosophical exposition requires. The objection has been raised by some recent editors of the work that faith receives disproportionate attention in the handbook, that the discussion of the other two virtues is fragmentary and hurried. "One looks, but in vain," it has been said, "for a discussion of charity more or less commensurate with that on Faith." [20] Yet, if one will take the trouble to observe how consistently the practical and productive spheres are subordinated to the theoretic sphere in all the great systematic expositions of secular philosophic science,[21] the methodological appropriateness of St. Augus-

[20] Arand, *op. cit.*, p. 6.
[21] In Hegel's *Enzyklopädie der philosophischen Wissenschaften*, for instance, the expositions of the "practical" and "productive" sciences, though very important, constitute only a part of the third division of the entire system.

tine's procedure in the *Enchiridion* at once becomes apparent. Over and above a content
peculiar to itself, theoretic or explanatory knowledge of necessity includes a theoretic account of
all that pertains both to the practical sphere of
human behavior and to the productive sphere of
human making. Similarly faith, which informs
the Christian intellect with knowledge of many
kinds of things, good and evil, near and far, past,
present and future, informs it also of the rela-
tively few things, of personal concern, which are
to be hoped for and loved, as well as feared and
hated. It is no wonder, therefore, that so many
chapters of the Augustinian handbook are devoted to exhibiting the objects of faith. Indeed,
strictly speaking, the entire work, including the
explicit discussions of hope and love, is explanatory, and, therefore, theoretical in character.

But, of course, as St. Augustine says, it is one
thing to be taught what is to be hoped for and
loved, and quite another actually to hope and
love. Faith believes, hope and love pray. Yet
belief that does not flower into prayer, faith
that does not flow into hope and work with love,
is dead faith. Thus, if the faith expounded at
length is living, it of necessity includes hope;
and love surely is expounded with it, for love
is the life of faith and the inspiration of hope.
Indeed, living faith and hope are, in a sense,
simply temporal aspects of true love. Insofar as
Christian love is directed toward union with
Omnipotent God, a union which can be consummated only hereafter, it manifests itself in
this life primarily under the character of the

hope which faith possesses. Insofar as it is directed toward union with Christ the Head, a union which was possible on earth only for a brief period centuries ago, it manifests itself primarily under the character of faith. Only insofar as it is directed toward union with the Body of Christ, which is the Church as a whole, can it be even approximately consummated in this life; and then it manifests itself, both inwardly and outwardly, in that love of one another commanded of all the faithful, which binds and builds the Christian community on earth.[22]

In the concluding paragraphs of the *Enchiridion*, St. Augustine masterfully returns to the contrast between the two loves—*cupiditas* of the natural order, *caritas* of the order of grace —upon which his entire system of thought depends. Of the experience of the Christian born in the natural order but destined to pass altogether into the order of grace, St. Augustine writes:

Lust diminishes [*diminuitur cupiditas*], as love grows [*caritate crescente*], till the latter grows to such a height that it can grow no higher here. For "greater love hath no man than this, that a man lay down his life for his friends." Who can tell how great love shall be in the future world, when there shall be no lust for it to restrain and conquer? for that will be the perfection of health when there shall be no struggle with death.

The English version of the *Enchiridion* used in the present edition is that of J. B. Shaw, which,

[22] For a detailed analysis of the place of the three theological virtues in St. Augustine's idea of the Church, see Fritz Hofmann, *Der Kirchenbegriff des Hl. Augustinus* (München, 1933), pp. 172-95.

of the many that exist, is perhaps the most idiomatic and accurate. To bring it into closer accord with the standard text of the original edited by O. Scheel in 1903,[23] some minor changes and corrections have been added to those already introduced by Philip Schaff in his *Select Library of the Nicene and Post-Nicene Fathers of the Christian Church*, published in 1900.[24] The division into 122 chapters adopted by Shaw from the text in the Migne collection has been retained, however, without superimposing upon it, as Scheel does, the division used in the Maurist edition.[25]

In the Appendix we have reprinted Adolph von Harnack's detailed analysis and very instructive historical appraisal of the work, which sums up his long exposition of Augustinian thought in the *History of Dogma*.[26]

[23] O. Scheel, *Augustins Enchiridion* (Tübingen and Leipzig, 1903).

[24] J. B. Shaw, trans., *The Enchiridion*, in *A Select Library of Nicene and Post-Nicene Fathers of the Christian Church*, ed. by Philip Schaff (New York, 1900), Vol. III, pp. 237-76.

[25] Scheel, *op. cit.*, p. x.

[26] Harnack, *op. cit.*, pp. 95, 104, and 222-39.

THE ENCHIRIDION
ON FAITH, HOPE AND LOVE

ARGUMENT

Laurentius having asked Augustine to furnish him with a handbook of Christian doctrine, containing in brief compass answers to several questions which he had proposed, Augustine shows him that these questions can be fully answered by any one who knows the proper objects of faith, hope, and love. He then proceeds, in the first part of the work (Chap. IX-CXIII), to expound the objects of faith, taking as his text the Apostles' Creed; and in the course of this exposition, besides refuting divers heresies, he throws out many observations on the conduct of life. The second part of the work (Chap. CXIV-CXVI) treats of the objects of hope, and consists of a very brief exposition of the several petitions in the Lord's Prayer. The third and concluding part (Chap. CXVII-CXXII) treats of the objects of love, showing the pre-eminence of this grace in the gospel system, that it is the end of the commandment and the fulfilling of the law, and that God Himself is love.

I. THE AUTHOR DESIRES THE GIFT OF TRUE WISDOM FOR LAURENTIUS

I CANNOT express, my beloved son Laurentius, the delight with which I witness your progress in knowledge, and the earnest desire I have that you should be a wise man: not one of those of whom it is said, "Where is the wise? where is the scribe? where is the disputer of this world? hath not God made foolish the wisdom of this world?" [1] but one of those of whom it is said, "The multitude of the wise is the welfare of the world," [2] and such as the apostle wishes those to become, whom he tells, "I would have you wise unto that which is good, and simple concerning evil." [3] [Now, just as no one can exist of himself, so no one can be wise of himself, but only by the enlightening influence of Him of whom it is written, "All wisdom cometh from the Lord."] [4]

II. THE FEAR OF GOD IS MAN'S TRUE WISDOM

The true wisdom of man is piety. You find this in the book of holy Job. For we read there what wisdom itself has said to man: "Behold, the fear of the Lord [*pietas*], that is wisdom." [5] If you ask further what is meant in that place by *pietas*, the Greek calls it more definitely θεοσέβεια, that is, the worship of God. The Greeks sometimes call piety εὐσέβεια, which signifies right worship, though this, of course, refers specially to the worship of God. But when we are defining in what man's true wisdom consists, the most convenient word to use is that which distinctly expresses the fear of God. And can you, who are anxious that I should treat of great matters in few words, wish for a briefer form of expression?

[1] 1 Cor. i. 20
[2] Wisd. vi. 24
[3] Rom. xvi. 19
[4] This sentence is not found in the older manuscripts and is omitted in the text of O. Scheel. Scriptural ref., Eccles. 1. 1. [Ed. note.]
[5] Job xxviii. 28

Or perhaps you are anxious that this expression should itself be briefly explained, and that I should unfold in a short discourse the proper mode of worshipping God?

III. GOD IS TO BE WORSHIPPED THROUGH FAITH, HOPE, AND LOVE

Now if I should answer, that God is to be worshipped with faith, hope, and love, you will at once say that this answer is too brief, and will ask me briefly to unfold the objects of each of these three graces, *viz.*, what we are to believe, what we are to hope for, and what we are to love. And when I have done this, you will have an answer to all the questions you asked in your letter. If you have kept a copy of your letter, you can easily turn it up and read it over again: if you have not, you will have no difficulty in recalling it when I refresh your memory.

IV. THE QUESTIONS PROPOUNDED BY LAURENTIUS

You are anxious, you say, that I should write a sort of handbook for you, which you might always keep beside you, containing answers to the questions you put, *viz.*: what ought to be man's chief end in life; what he ought, in view of the various heresies, chiefly to avoid; to what extent religion is supported by reason; what there is in reason that lends no support to faith, when faith stands alone; what is the starting-point, what the goal, of religion; what is the sum of the whole body of doctrine; what is the sure and proper foundation of the Catholic Faith. Now, undoubtedly, you will know the answers to all these questions, if you know thoroughly the proper objects of faith, hope, and love. For these must be the chief, nay, the exclusive objects of pursuit in religion. He who speaks against these is either a total stranger to the name of Christ, or is a heretic. These are to be defended by reason, which must have its starting-point either in the bodily senses or in the intuitions of the mind. And what we have neither had experience of through our bodily senses, nor have been able to reach through the intellect, must undoubtedly be believed on the testimony of those witnesses by whom the Scriptures, justly called divine, were written; and who by divine assistance were enabled, either through bodily sense or intellectual perception, to see or to foresee the things in question.

V. Brief Answers to These Questions

Moreover, when the mind has been imbued with the first elements of that faith which worketh by love,[6] it endeavors by purity of life to attain unto sight, where the pure and perfect in heart know that unspeakable beauty, the full vision of which is supreme happiness. Here surely is an answer to your question as to what

[6] Gal. v. 6

is the starting-point, and what the goal: we begin
in faith, and are made perfect by sight. This also
is the sum of the whole body of doctrine. But
the sure and proper foundation of the Catholic
Faith is Christ. "For other foundation," says the
apostle, "can no man lay than that is laid, which
is Jesus Christ." [7] Nor are we to deny that this
is the proper foundation of the Catholic Faith,
because it may be supposed that some heretics
hold this in common with us. For if we carefully
consider the things that pertain to Christ, we
shall find that, among those heretics who call
themselves Christians, Christ is present in name
only: in deed and in truth He is not among
them. But to show this would occupy us too long,
for we should require to go over all the heresies
which have existed, which do exist, or which
could exist, under the Christian name, and to
show that this is true in the case of each—a discussion which would occupy so many volumes
as to be all but interminable.

VI. Controversy Out of Place in a Handbook Like the Present

Now you ask of me a handbook, that is, one
that can be carried in the hand, not one to load
your shelves. To return, then, to the three graces
through which, as I have said, God should be
worshipped—faith, hope, and love: to state what
are the true and proper objects of each of these
is easy. But to defend this true doctrine against

[7] 1 Cor. iii. 11

the assaults of those who hold an opposite opinion, requires much fuller and more elaborate instruction. And the true way to obtain this instruction is not to have a short treatise put into one's hands, but to have a great zeal kindled in one's heart.

VII. The Creed and the Lord's Prayer Demand the Exercise of Faith, Hope, and Love

For you have the Creed and the Lord's Prayer. What can be briefer to hear or to read? What easier to commit to memory? When, as the result of sin, the human race was groaning under a heavy load of misery, and was in urgent need of the divine compassion, one of the prophets, anticipating the time of God's grace, declared: "And it shall come to pass, that whosoever shall call on the name of the Lord shall be delivered." [8] Hence the Lord's Prayer. But the apostle, when, for the purpose of commending this very grace, he had quoted this prophetic testimony, immediately added: "How then shall they call on Him in whom they have not believed?" [9] Hence the Creed. In these two you have those three graces exemplified: faith believes, hope and love pray. But without faith the two last cannot exist, and therefore we may say that faith also prays. Whence it is written: "How shall they call on Him in whom they have not believed?"

[8] Joel ii. 32
[9] Rom. x. 14

VIII. The Distinction Between Faith and Hope, and the Mutual Dependence of Faith, Hope, and Love

Again, can anything be hoped for which is not an object of faith? It is true that a thing which is not an object of hope may be believed. What true Christian, for example, does not believe in the punishment of the wicked? And yet such an one does not hope for it. And the man who believes that punishment to be hanging over himself, and who shrinks in horror from the prospect, is more properly said to fear than to hope. And these two states of mind the poet carefully distinguishes, when he says: "Permit the fearful to have hope." [10] Another poet, who is usually much superior to this one, makes a wrong use of the word, when he says: "If I have been able to hope for so great a grief as this." [11] And some grammarians take this case as an example of impropriety of speech, saying, "He said *sperare* [to hope] instead of *timere* [to fear]." Accordingly, faith may have for its object evil as well as good; for both good and evil are believed, and the faith that believes them is not evil, but good. Faith, moreover, is concerned with the past, the present, and the future, all three. We believe, for example, that Christ died —an event in the past; we believe that He is sitting at the right hand of God—a state of things

[10] Lucan, *Phars.* ii. 15
[11] Virgil, *Aen.* iv. 419

which is present; we believe that He will come
to judge the quick and the dead—an event of the
future. Again, faith applies both to one's own
circumstances and those of others. Every one,
for example, believes that his own existence had
a beginning, and was not eternal, and he believes
the same both of other men and other things.
Many of our beliefs in regard to religious matters,
again, have reference not merely to other men,
but to angels also. But hope has for its object only
what is good, only what is future, and only what
affects the man who entertains the hope. For
these reasons, then, faith must be distinguished
from hope, not merely as a matter of verbal
propriety, but because they are essentially different. The fact that we do not see either what
we believe or what we hope for, is all that is
common to faith and hope. In the *Epistle to the
Hebrews*, for example, faith is defined (and
eminent defenders of the Catholic Faith have
used the definition as a standard) "the evidence
of things not seen." [12] Although, should any one
say that he believes, that is, has grounded his
faith, not on words, nor on witnesses, nor on
any reasoning whatever, but on the direct evidence of his own senses, he would not be guilty
of such an impropriety of speech as to be justly
liable to the criticism, "You saw, therefore you
did not believe." And hence it does not follow
that an object of faith is not an object of sight.
But it is better that we should use the word
"faith" as the Scriptures have taught us, applying
it to those things which are not seen. Concerning

[12] Heb. xi. 1

hope, again, the apostle says: "Hope that is seen
is not hope; for what a man seeth, why doth he
yet hope for? But if we hope for that we see not,
then do we with patience wait for it." [13] When,
then, we believe that good is about to come, this
is nothing else but to hope for it. Now what shall
I say of love? Without it, faith profits nothing;
and in its absence, hope cannot exist. The Apostle
James says: "The devils also believe, and trem-
ble" [14]—that is, they, having neither hope nor
love, but believing that what we love and hope
for is about to come, are in terror. And so the
Apostle Paul approves and commends the "faith
that worketh by love;" [15] and this certainly cannot exist without hope. Wherefore there is no
love without hope, no hope without love, and
neither love nor hope without faith.

IX. What We Are to Believe. In Regard to
Nature It Is Not Necessary for the
Christian to Know More Than That
the Goodness of the Creator Is the
Cause of All Things

When, then, the question is asked what we are
to believe in regard to religion, it is not necessary
to probe into the nature of things, as was done
by those whom the Greeks call *physici;* nor need
we be in alarm lest the Christian should be ignorant of the force and number of the elements

[13] Rom. viii. 24, 25
[14] Jas. ii. 19
[15] Gal. v. 6

—the motion, and order, and eclipses of the heavenly bodies; the form of the heavens; the species and the natures of animals, plants, stones, fountains, rivers, mountains; about chronology and distances; the signs of coming storms; and a thousand other things which those philosophers either have found out, or think they have found out. For even these men themselves, endowed though they are with so much genius, burning with zeal, abounding in leisure, tracking some things by the aid of human conjecture, searching into others with the aids of history and experience, have not found out all things; and even their boasted discoveries are oftener mere guesses than certain knowledge. It is enough for the Christian to believe that the only cause of all created things, whether heavenly or earthly, whether visible or invisible, is the goodness of the Creator, the one true God; and that nothing exists but Himself that does not derive its existence from Him; and that He is the Trinity—to wit, the Father, and the Son begotten of the Father, and the Holy Spirit proceeding from the same Father, but one and the same Spirit of Father and Son.

X. The Supremely Good Creator Made All Things Good

By the Trinity, thus supremely and equally and unchangeably good, all things were created; and these are not supremely and equally and unchangeably good, but yet they are good, even taken separately. Taken as a whole, however, they are very good, because their *ensemble* constitutes the universe in all its wonderful order and beauty.

XI. WHAT IS CALLED EVIL IN THE UNIVERSE IS BUT THE ABSENCE OF GOOD

And in the universe, even that which is called evil, when it is regulated and put in its own place, only enhances our admiration of the good; for we enjoy and value the good more when we compare it with the evil. For the Almighty God, who, as even the heathen acknowledge, has supreme power over all things, being Himself supremely good, would never permit the existence of anything evil among His works, if He were not so omnipotent and good that He can bring good even out of evil. For what is that which we call evil but the absence of good? In the bodies of animals, disease and wounds mean nothing but the absence of health; for when a cure is effected, that does not mean that the evils which were present—namely, the diseases and wounds—go away from the body and dwell elsewhere: they altogether cease to exist; for the wound or disease is not a substance, but a defect in the fleshly substance—the flesh itself being a substance, and therefore something good, of which those evils—that is, privations of the good which we call health—are accidents. Just in the same way, what are called vices in the soul are

nothing but privations of natural good. And
when they are cured, they are not transferred
elsewhere: when they cease to exist in the healthy
soul, they cannot exist anywhere else.

XII. ALL BEINGS WERE MADE GOOD, BUT NOT BEING MADE PERFECTLY GOOD, ARE LIABLE TO CORRUPTION

All things that exist, therefore, seeing that the
Creator of them all is supremely good, are themselves good. But because they are not, like their
Creator, supremely and unchangeably good, their
good may be diminished and increased. But for
good to be diminished is an evil, although, however much it may be diminished, it is necessary,
if the being is to continue, that some good should
remain to constitute the being. For however
small or of whatever kind the being may be, the
good which makes it a being cannot be destroyed
without destroying the being itself. An uncor-
rupted nature is justly held in esteem. But if,
still further, it be incorruptible, it is undoubtedly
considered of still higher value. When it is corrupted, however, its corruption is an evil, because
it is deprived of some sort of good. For if it be
deprived of no good, it receives no injury; but
it does receive injury, therefore it is deprived
of good. Therefore, so long as a being is in
process of corruption, there is in it some good
of which it is being deprived; and if a part of the
being should remain which cannot be corrupted,

this will certainly be an incorruptible being, and accordingly the process of corruption will result in the manifestation of this great good. But if it do not cease to be corrupted, neither can it cease to possess good of which corruption may deprive it. But if it should be thoroughly and completely consumed by corruption, there will then be no good left, because there will be no being. Wherefore corruption can consume the good only by consuming the being. Every being, therefore, is a good; a great good, if it cannot be corrupted; a little good, if it can: but in any case, only the foolish or ignorant will deny that it is a good. And if it be wholly consumed by corruption, then the corruption itself must cease to exist, as there is no being left in which it can dwell.

XIII. There Can Be No Evil Where There Is No Good; and an Evil Man Is an Evil Good

Accordingly, there is nothing of what we call evil, if there be nothing good. But a good which is wholly without evil is a perfect good. A good, on the other hand, which contains evil is a faulty or imperfect good; and there can be no evil where there is no good. From all this we arrive at the curious result: that since every being, so far as it is a being, is good, when we say that a faulty being is an evil being, we just seem to say that what is good is evil, and that nothing but what is good can be evil, seeing that every being is good, and that no evil can exist except in a being. Nothing, then, can be evil except something which is good. And although this, when stated, seems to be a contradiction, yet the strictness of reasoning leaves us no escape from the conclusion. We must, however, beware of incurring the prophetic condemnation: "Woe unto them that call evil good, and good evil: that put darkness for light, and light for darkness: that put bitter for sweet, and sweet for bitter." [16] And yet our Lord says: "An evil man out of the evil treasure of his heart bringeth forth that which is evil." [17] Now, what is an evil man but an evil being? for a man is a being. Now, if a man is a good thing because he is a being, what is an evil man but an evil good? Yet, when we accurately distinguish these two things, we find that it is not because he is a man that he is an evil, or because he is wicked that he is a good; but that he is a good because he is a man, and an evil because he is wicked. Whoever, then, says, "To be a man is an evil," or, "To be wicked is a good," falls under the prophetic denunciation: "Woe unto them that call evil good, and good evil!" For he condemns the work of God, which is the man, and praises the defect of man, which is the wickedness. Therefore every being, even if it be a defective one, in so far as it is a being is good, and in so far as it is defective is evil.

[16] Isa. v. 20
[17] Luke vi. 45

XIV. Good and Evil Are an Exception to the Rule That Contrary Attributes Cannot Be Predicated of the Same Subject. Evil Springs Up in What Is Good, and Cannot Exist Except in What Is Good

Accordingly, in the case of these contraries which we call good and evil, the rule of the logicians, that two contraries cannot be predicated at the same time of the same thing, does not hold. No weather is at the same time dark and bright: no food or drink is at the same time sweet and bitter: no body is at the same time and in the same place black and white: none is at the same time and in the same place deformed and beautiful. And this rule is found to hold in regard to many, indeed nearly all, contraries, that they cannot exist at the same time in any one thing. But although no one can doubt that good and evil are contraries, not only can they exist at the same time, but evil cannot exist without good, or in anything that is not good. Good, however, can exist without evil. For a man or an angel can exist without being wicked; but nothing can be wicked except a man or an angel: and so far as he is a man or an angel, he is good; so far as he is wicked, he is an evil. And these two contraries are so far co-existent, that if good did not exist in what is evil, neither could evil exist; because corruption could not have either a place to dwell in, or a source to spring from, if there were nothing that could be corrupted;

and nothing can be corrupted except what is good, for corruption is nothing else but the destruction of good. From what is good, then, evils arose, and except in what is good they do not exist; nor was there any other source from which any evil nature could arise. For if there were, then, in so far as this was a being, it was certainly a good: and a being which was incorruptible would be a great good; and even one which was corruptible must be to some extent a good, for only by corrupting what was good in it could corruption do it harm.

XV. The Preceding Argument Is in No Wise Inconsistent With the Saying of Our Lord: "A Good Tree Cannot Bring Forth Evil Fruit"

But when we say that evil springs out of good, let it not be thought that this contradicts our Lord's saying: "A good tree cannot bring forth evil fruit." [18] For, as the Truth says, you cannot gather grapes of thorns,[19] because grapes do not grow on thorns. But we see that on good soil both vines and thorns may be grown. And in the same way, just as an evil tree cannot bring forth good fruit, so an evil will cannot produce good works. But from the nature of man, which is good, may spring either a good or an evil will. And certainly there was at first no source from which an evil will could spring, except the nature

[18] Matt. vii. 18
[19] Matt. vii. 16

of angel or of man, which was good. And our Lord Himself clearly shows this in the very same place where He speaks about the tree and its fruit. For He says: "Either make the tree good, and his fruit good; or else make the tree corrupt, and his fruit corrupt" [20]—clearly enough warning us that evil fruits do not grow on a good tree, nor good fruits on an evil tree; but that nevertheless the ground itself, by which He meant those whom He was then addressing, might grow either kind of trees.

XVI. It Is Not Essential to Man's Happiness That He Should Know the Causes of Physical Convulsions; but It Is, That He should Know the Causes of Good and Evil

Now, in view of these considerations, when we are pleased with that line of Maro, "Happy the man who has attained to the knowledge of the causes of things," [21] we should not suppose that it is necessary to happiness to know the causes of the great physical convulsions, causes which lie hid in the most secret recesses of nature's kingdom, "whence comes the earthquake whose force makes the deep seas to swell and burst their barriers, and again to return upon themselves and settle down." [22] But we ought to know the causes of good and evil as far as man may

[20] Matt. xii. 33
[21] Virgil, Georgics, ii. 490
[22] Ibid.

in this life know them, in order to avoid the mistakes and troubles of which this life is so full. For our aim must always be to reach that state of happiness in which no trouble shall distress us, and no error mislead us. If we must know the causes of physical convulsions, there are none which it concerns us more to know than those which affect our own health. But seeing that, in our ignorance of these, we are fain to resort to physicians, it would seem that we might bear with considerable patience our ignorance of the secrets that lie hid in the earth and heavens.

XVII. The Nature of Error. All Error Is Not Hurtful, Though It Is Man's Duty as Far as Possible to Avoid It

For although we ought with the greatest possible care to avoid error, not only in great but even in little things, and although we cannot err except through ignorance, it does not follow that, if a man is ignorant of a thing, he must forthwith fall into error. That is rather the fate of the man who thinks he knows what he does not know. For he accepts what is false as if it were true, and that is the essence of error. But it is a point of very great importance what the subject is in regard to which a man makes a mistake. For on one and the same subject we rightly prefer an instructed man to an ignorant one, and a man who is not in error to one who is. In the case of different subjects, however—

that is, when one man knows one thing, and
another a different thing, and when what the
former knows is useful, and what the latter
knows is not so useful, or is actually hurtful—
who would not, in regard to the things the
latter knows, prefer the ignorance of the former
to the knowledge of the latter? For there are
points on which ignorance is better than knowledge. And in the same way, it has sometimes
been an advantage to depart from the right way
—in travelling, however, not in morals. It has
happened to myself to take the wrong road where
two ways met, so that I did not pass by the
place where an armed band of Donatists lay
in wait for me. Yet I arrived at the place whither
I was bent, though by a roundabout route;
and when I heard of the ambush, I congratu-
lated myself on my mistake, and gave thanks
to God for it. Now, who would not rather be
the traveller who made a mistake like this, than
the highwayman who made no mistake? And
hence, perhaps, it is that the prince of poets
puts these words into the mouth of a lover in
misery:[23] "How I am undone, how I have been
carried away by an evil error!" for there is an
error which is good, as it not merely does no
harm, but produces some actual advantage. But
when we look more closely into the nature of
truth, and consider that to err is just to take
the false for the true, and the true for the false,
or to hold what is certain as uncertain, and
what is uncertain as certain, and that error in
the soul is hideous and repulsive just in propor-

[23] Virgil, *Eclog.* viii. 41

tion as it appears fair and plausible when we utter it, or assent to it, saying, "Yea, yea; Nay, nay"—surely this life that we live is wretched indeed, if only on this account, that sometimes, in order to preserve it, it is necessary to fall into error. God forbid that such should be that other life, where truth itself is the life of the soul, where no one deceives, and no one is deceived. But here men deceive and are deceived, and they are more to be pitied when they lead others astray than when they are themselves led astray by putting trust in liars. Yet so much does a rational soul shrink from what is false, and so earnestly does it struggle against error, that even those who love to deceive are most unwilling to be deceived. For the liar does not think that he errs, but that he leads another who trusts him into error. And certainly he does not err in regard to the matter about which he lies, if he himself knows the truth; but he is deceived in this, that he thinks his lie does him no harm, whereas every sin is more hurtful to the sinner than to the sinned against.

XVIII. It Is Never Allowable to Tell a Lie; but Lies Differ Very Much in Guilt, According to the Intention and the Subject

But here arises a very difficult and very intricate question, about which I once wrote a large book, finding it necessary to give it an answer. The question is this: whether at any time it can

become the duty of a good man to tell a lie? For
some go so far as to contend that there are
occasions on which it is a good and pious work
to commit perjury even, and to say what is false
about matters that relate to the worship of God,
and about the very nature of God Himself. To
me, however, it seems certain that every lie is
a sin, though it makes a great difference with
what intention and on what subject one lies.
For the sin of the man who tells a lie to help
another is not so heinous as that of the man who
tells a lie to injure another; and the man who by
his lying puts a traveller on the wrong road,
does not do so much harm as the man who by
false or misleading representations distorts the
whole course of a life. No one, of course, is to
be condemned as a liar who says what is false,
believing it to be true, because such an one
does not consciously deceive, but rather is himself deceived. And, on the same principle, a
man is not to be accused of lying, though he
may sometimes be open to the charge of rashness,
if through carelessness he takes up what is false
and holds it as true; but, on the other hand, the
man who says what is true, believing it to be
false, is, so far as his own consciousness is concerned, a liar. For in saying what he does not
believe, he says what to his own conscience is
false, even though it should in fact be true; nor
is the man in any sense free from lying who with
his mouth speaks the truth without knowing it,
but in his heart wills to tell a lie. And, therefore,
not looking at the matter spoken of, but solely
at the intention of the speaker, the man who

unwittingly says what is false, thinking all the
time that it is true, is a better man than the one
who unwittingly says what is true, but in his
conscience intends to deceive. For the former
does not think one thing and say another; but
the latter, though his statements may be true in
fact, has one thought in his heart and another
on his lips: and that is the very essence of lying.
But when we come to consider truth and falsehood in respect to the subjects spoken of, the
point on which one deceives or is deceived
becomes a matter of the utmost importance. For
although, as far as a man's own conscience is
concerned, it is a greater evil to deceive than to
be deceived, nevertheless it is a far less evil
to tell a lie in regard to matters that do not relate
to religion, than to be led into error in regard
to matters the knowledge and belief of which
are essential to the right worship of God. To
illustrate this by example: suppose that one man
should say of some one who is dead that he is
still alive, knowing this to be untrue; and that
another man should, being deceived, believe that
Christ shall at the end of some time (make the
time as long as you please) die; would it not
be incomparably better to lie like the former,
than to be deceived like the latter? and would
it not be a much less evil to lead some man into
the former error, than to be led by any man into
the latter?

XIX. Men's Errors Vary Very Much in the Magnitude of the Evils They Produce; but Yet Every Error Is in Itself an Evil

In some things, then, it is a great evil to be deceived; in some it is a small evil; in some no evil at all; and in some it is an actual advantage. It is to his grievous injury that a man is deceived when he does not believe what leads to eternal life, or believes what leads to eternal death. It is a small evil for a man to be deceived, when, by taking falsehood for truth, he brings upon himself temporal annoyances; for the patience of the believer will turn even these to a good use, as when, for example, taking a bad man for a good, he receives injury from him. But one who believes a bad man to be good, and yet suffers no injury, is nothing the worse for being deceived, nor does he fall under the prophetic denunciation: "Woe to those who call evil good!" [24] For we are to understand that this is spoken not about evil man, but about the things that make men evil. Hence the man who calls adultery good, falls justly under that prophetic denunciation. But the man who calls the adulterer good, thinking him to be chaste, and not knowing him to be an adulterer, falls into no error in regard to the nature of good and evil, but only makes a mistake as to the secrets of human con-

[24] Isa. v. 20

duct. He calls the man good on the ground of believing him to be what is undoubtedly good; he calls the adulterer evil, and the pure man good; and he calls this man good, not knowing him to be an adulterer, but believing him to be pure. Further, if by making a mistake one escape death, as I have said above once happened to me, one even derives some advantage from one's mistake. But when I assert that in certain cases a man may be deceived without any injury to himself, or even with some advantage to himself, I do not mean that the mistake in itself is no evil, or is in any sense a good; I refer only to the evil that is avoided, or the advantage that is gained, through making the mistake. For the mistake, considered in itself, is an evil: a great evil if it concern a great matter, a small evil if it concern a small matter, but yet always an evil. For who that is of sound mind can deny that it is an evil to receive what is false as if it were true, and to reject what is true as if it were false, or to hold what is uncertain as certain, and what is certain as uncertain? But it is one thing to think a man good when he is really bad, which is a mistake; it is another thing to suffer no ulterior injury in consequence of the mistake, supposing that the bad man whom we think good inflicts no damage upon us. In the same way, it is one thing to think that we are on the right road when we are not; it is another thing when this mistake of ours, which is an evil, leads to some good, such as saving us from an ambush of wicked men.

XX. Every Error Is Not a Sin. An Examination of the Opinion of the Academic Philosophers, That to Avoid Error We Should in All Cases Suspend Belief

I am not sure whether mistakes such as the following—when one forms a good opinion of a bad man, not knowing what sort of man he is; or when, instead of the ordinary perceptions through the bodily senses, other appearances of a similar kind present themselves, which we perceive in the spirit, but think we perceive in the body, or perceive in the body, but think we perceive in the spirit (such a mistake as the Apostle Peter made when the angel suddenly freed him from his chains and imprisonment, and he thought he saw a vision[25]); or when, in the case of sensible objects themselves, we mistake rough for smooth, or bitter for sweet, or think that putrid matter has a good smell; or when we mistake the passing of a carriage for thunder; or mistake one man for another, the two being very much alike, as often happens in the case of twins (hence our great poet calls it "a mistake pleasing to parents"[26])—whether these, and other mistakes of this kind, ought to be called sins. Nor do I now undertake to solve a very knotty question, which perplexed those very acute thinkers, the Academic philosophers: whether a wise man ought to give his assent to

[25] Acts xii. 9
[26] Virgil, *Aen.* x. 392

anything, seeing that he may fall into error by assenting to falsehood: for all things, as they assert, are either unknown or uncertain. Now I wrote three volumes shortly after my conversion, to remove out of my way the objections which lie, as it were, on the very threshold of faith. And assuredly it was necessary at the very outset to remove this utter despair of reaching truth, which seems to be strengthened by the arguments of these philosophers. Now in their eyes every error is regarded as a sin, and they think that error can only be avoided by entirely suspending belief. For they say that the man who assents to what is uncertain falls into error; and they strive by the most acute, but most audacious arguments, to show that, even though a man's opinion should by chance be true, yet that there is no certainty of its truth, owing to the impossibility of distinguishing truth from falsehood. But with us, "the just shall live by faith." [27] Now, if assent be taken away, faith goes too; for without assent there can be no belief. And there are truths, whether we know them or not, which must be believed if we would attain to a happy life, that is, to eternal life. But I am not sure whether one ought to argue with men who not only do not know that there is an eternal life before them, but do not know whether they are living at the present moment; nay, say that they do not know what it is impossible they can be ignorant of. For it is impossible that any one should be ignorant that he is alive, seeing that if he be not alive it is impossible for him to be

[27] Rom. i. 17

ignorant; for not knowledge merely, but ignorance too, can be an attribute only of the living. But, forsooth, they think that by not acknowledging that they are alive they avoid error, when even their very error proves that they are alive, since one who is not alive cannot err. As, then, it is not only true, but certain, that we are alive, so there are many other things both true and certain; and God forbid that it should ever be called wisdom, and not the height of folly, to refuse assent to these.

XXI. Error, Though Not Always a Sin, Is Always an Evil

But as to those matters in regard to which our belief or disbelief, and indeed their truth or supposed truth or falsity, are of no importance whatever, so far as attaining the kingdom of God is concerned: to make a mistake in such matters is not to be looked on as a sin, or at least as a very small and trifling sin. In short, a mistake in matters of this kind, whatever its nature and magnitude, does not relate to the way of approach to God, which is the faith of Christ that "worketh by love." [28] For the "mistake pleasing to parents" in the case of the twin children was no deviation from this way; nor did the Apostle Peter deviate from this way, when, thinking that he saw a vision, he so mistook one thing for another, that, till the angel who delivered him had departed from him, he did not distin-

[28] Gal. v. 6

guish the real objects among which he was
moving from the visionary objects of a dream;[29]
nor did the patriarch Jacob deviate from this
way, when he believed that his son, who was
really alive, had been slain by a beast.[30] In the
case of these and other false impressions of the
same kind, we are indeed deceived, but our faith
in God remains secure. We go astray, but we do
not leave the way that leads us to Him. But yet
these errors, though they are not sinful, are to
be reckoned among the evils of this life, which
is so far made subject to vanity, that we receive
what is false as if it were true, reject what is true
as if it were false, and cling to what is uncertain
as if it were certain. And although they do not
trench upon that true and certain faith through
which we reach eternal blessedness, yet they
have much to do with that misery in which we
are now living. And assuredly, if we were now
in the enjoyment of the true and perfect happiness that lies before us, we should not be subject
to any deception through any sense, whether of
body or of mind.

XXII. A Lie Is Not Allowable, Even to Save Another From Injury

But every lie must be called a sin, because
not only when a man knows the truth, but even
when, as a man may be, he is mistaken and
deceived, it is his duty to say what he thinks in

[29] Acts xii. 9-11
[30] Gen. xxxvii. 33

his heart, whether it be true, or whether he only think it to be true. But every liar says the opposite of what he thinks in his heart, with purpose to deceive. Now it is evident that speech was given to man, not that men might therewith deceive one another, but that one man might make known his thoughts to another. To use speech, then, for the purpose of deception, and not for its appointed end, is a sin. Nor are we to suppose that there is any lie that is not a sin, because it is sometimes possible, by telling a lie, to do service to another. For it is possible to do this by theft also, as when we steal from a rich man who never feels the loss, to give to a poor man who is sensibly benefited by what he gets. And the same can be said of adultery also, when, for instance, some woman appears likely to die of love unless we consent to her wishes, while if she lived she might purify herself by repentance; but yet no one will assert that on this account such an adultery is not a sin. And if we justly place so high a value upon chastity, what offense have we taken at truth, that, while no prospect of advantage to another will lead us to violate the former by adultery, we should be ready to violate the latter by lying? It cannot be denied that they have attained a very high standard of goodness who never lie except to save a man from injury; but in the case of men who have reached this standard, it is not the deceit, but their good intention, that is justly praised, and sometimes even rewarded. It is quite enough that the deception should be pardoned, without its being made an object of laudation, especially

among the heirs of the new covenant, to whom
it is said: "Let your communication be, Yea,
yea; Nay, nay: for whatsoever is more than
these cometh of evil." [31] And it is on account of
this evil, which never ceases to creep in while
we retain this mortal vesture, that the co-heirs
of Christ themselves say, "Forgive us our debts." [32]

XXIII. Summary of the Results of the Preceding Discussion

As it is right that we should know the causes
of good and evil, so much of them at least as
will suffice for the way that leads us to the kingdom, where there will be life without the shadow
of death, truth without any alloy of error, and
happiness unbroken by any sorrow, I have discussed these subjects with the brevity which
my limited space demanded. And I think there
cannot now be any doubt, that the only cause
of any good that we enjoy is the goodness of
God, and that the only cause of evil is the falling
away from the unchangeable good of a being
made good but changeable, first in the case of an
angel, and afterwards in the case of man.

XXIV. The Secondary Causes of Evil Are Ignorance and Lust

This is the first evil that befell the intelligent
creation—that is, its first privation of good.

[31] Matt. v. 37
[32] Matt. vi. 12

Following upon this crept in, and now even in opposition to man's will, *ignorance* of duty, and *lust* after what is hurtful: and these brought in their train *error* and *suffering*, which, when they are felt to be imminent, produce that shrinking of the mind which is called *fear*. Further, when the mind attains the objects of its desire, however hurtful or empty they may be, error prevents it from perceiving their true nature, or its perceptions are overborne by a diseased appetite, and so it is puffed up with a *foolish joy*. From these fountains of evil, which spring out of defect rather than superfluity, flows every form of misery that besets a rational nature.

XXV. God's Judgments upon Fallen Men and Angels. The Death of the Body Is Man's Peculiar Punishment

And yet such a nature, in the midst of all its evils, could not lose the craving after happiness. Now the evils I have mentioned are common to all who for their wickedness have been justly condemned by God, whether they be men or angels. But there is one form of punishment peculiar to man—the death of the body. God had threatened him with this punishment of death if he should sin,[33] leaving him indeed to the freedom of his own will, but yet commanding his obedience under pain of death; and He placed him amid the happiness of Eden, as it were in a protected nook of life, with the intention that,

[33] Gen. ii. 17

if he preserved his righteousness, he should thence ascend to a better place.

XXVI. Through Adam's Sin His Whole Posterity Were Corrupted, and Were Born Under the Penalty of Death, Which He Had Incurred

Thence, after his sin, he was driven into exile, and by his sin the whole race of which he was the root was corrupted in him, and thereby subjected to the penalty of death. And so it happens that all descended from him, and from the woman who had led him into sin, and was condemned at the same time with him—being the offspring of carnal lust on which the same punishment of disobedience was visited—were tainted with the original sin, and were by it drawn through divers errors and sufferings into that last and endless punishment which they suffer in common with the fallen angels, their corrupters and masters, and the partakers of their doom. And thus "by one man sin entered into the world, and death by sin; and so death passed upon all men, for that all have sinned." [34] By "the world" the apostle, of course, means in this place the whole human race.

[34] Rom. v. 12

XXVII. The State of Misery to Which Adam's Sin Reduced Mankind, and the Restoration Effected Through the Mercy of God

Thus, then, matters stood. The whole mass of the human race was under condemnation, was lying steeped and wallowing in misery, and was being tossed from one form of evil to another, and, having joined the faction of the fallen angels, was paying the well-merited penalty of that impious rebellion. For whatever the wicked freely do through blind and unbridled lust, and whatever they suffer against their will in the way of open punishment, this all evidently pertains to the just wrath of God. But the goodness of the Creator never fails either to supply life and vital power to the wicked angels (without which their existence would soon come to an end); or, in the case of mankind, who spring from a condemned and corrupt stock, to impart form and life to their seed, to fashion their members, and through the various seasons of their life, and in the different parts of the earth, to quicken their senses, and bestow upon them the nourishment they need. For He judged it better to bring good out of evil, than not to permit any evil to exist. And if He had determined that in the case of men, as in the case of the fallen angels, there should be no restoration to happiness, would it not have been quite just, that the being who rebelled against God, who

in the abuse of his freedom spurned and trans-
gressed the command of his Creator when he
could so easily have kept it, who defaced in
himself the image of his Creator by stubbornly
turning away from His light, who by an evil use
of his free-will broke away from his wholesome
bondage to the Creator's laws—would it not have
been just that such a being should have been
wholly and to all eternity deserted by God, and
left to suffer the everlasing punishment he had
so richly earned? Certainly so God would have
done, had He been only just and not also
merciful, and had He not designed that His
unmerited mercy should shine forth the more
brightly in contrast with the unworthiness of its
objects.

XXVIII. When the Rebellious Angels Were Cast Out, the Rest Remained in the Enjoyment of Eternal Happiness With God

While some of the angels, then, in their pride
and impiety rebelled against God, and were cast
down from their heavenly abode into the lowest
darkness, the remaining number dwelt with God
in eternal and unchanging purity and happiness.
For all were not sprung from one angel who
had fallen and been condemned, so that they
were not all, like men, involved by one original
sin in the bonds of an inherited guilt, and so
made subject to the penalty which one had in-
curred; but when he, who afterwards became

the devil, was with his associates in crime exalted in pride, and by that very exaltation was with them cast down, the rest remained steadfast in piety and obedience to their Lord, and obtained, what before they had not enjoyed, a sure and certain knowledge of their eternal safety, and freedom from the possibility of falling.

XXIX. The Restored Part of Humanity Shall, in Accordance With the Promises of God, Succeed to the Place Which the Rebellious Angels Lost

And so it pleased God, the Creator and Governor of the universe, that, since the whole body of the angels had not fallen into rebellion, the part of them which had fallen should remain in perdition eternally, and that the other part, which had in the rebellion remained steadfastly loyal, should rejoice in the sure and certain knowledge of their eternal happiness; but that, on the other hand, mankind, who constituted the remainder of the intelligent creation, having perished without exception under sin, both original and actual, and the consequent punishments, should be in part restored, and should fill up the gap which the rebellion and fall of the devils had left in the company of the angels. For this is the promise to the saints, that at the resurrection they shall be equal to the angels of God.[35] And thus the Jerusalem which is above, which is the mother of us all, the city of God,

[35] Luke xx. 36

shall not be spoiled of any of the number of
her citizens, shall perhaps reign over even a
more abundant population. We do not know the
number either of the saints or of the devils;
but we know that the children of the holy mother
who was called barren on earth shall succeed
to the place of the fallen angels, and shall dwell
for ever in that peaceful abode from which
they fell. But the number of the citizens, whether
as it now is or as it shall be, is present to the
thoughts of the great Creator, who calls those
things which are not as though they were,[36]
and ordereth all things in measure, and number,
and weight.[37]

XXX. Men Are Not Saved by Good Works, Nor by the Free Determination of Their Own Will, but by the Grace of God Through Faith

But this part of the human race to which God
has promised pardon and a share in His eternal
kingdom, can they be restored through the merit
of their own works? God forbid. For what good
work can a lost man perform, except so far as
he has been delivered from perdition? Can they
do anything by the free determination of their
own will? Again I say, God forbid. For it was by
the evil use of his free-will that man destroyed
both it and himself. For, as a man who kills
himself must, of course, be alive when he kills

[36] Rom. iv. 17
[37] Wisd. xi. 20

himself, but after he has killed himself ceases
to live, and cannot restore himself to life; so,
when man by his own free-will sinned, then sin
being victorious over him, the freedom of his
will was lost. "For of whom a man is overcome,
of the same is he brought in bondage." [38] This
is the judgment of the Apostle Peter. And as it
is certainly true, what kind of liberty, I ask, can
the bond-slave possess, except when it pleases
him to sin? For he is freely in bondage who does
with pleasure the will of his master. Accordingly,
he who is the servant of sin is free to sin. And
hence he will not be free to do right, until,
being freed from sin, he shall begin to be the
servant of righteousness. And this is true liberty,
for he has pleasure in the righteous deed; and
it is at the same time a holy bondage, for he is
obedient to the will of God. But whence comes
this liberty to do right to the man who is in
bondage and sold under sin, except he be redeemed by Him who has said, "If the Son shall
make you free, ye shall be free indeed"? [39] And
before this redemption is wrought in a man, when
he is not yet free to do what is right, how can
he talk of the freedom of his will and his good
works, except he be inflated by that foolish
pride of boasting which the apostle restrains
when he says, "By grace are ye saved, through
faith." [40]

[38] 2 Pet. ii. 19
[39] John viii. 36
[40] Eph. ii. 8

XXXI. Faith Itself Is the Gift of God; and Good Works Will Not Be Wanting in Those Who Believe

And lest men should arrogate to themselves the merit of their own faith at least, not understanding that this too is the gift of God, this same apostle, who says in another place that he had "obtained mercy of the Lord to be faithful," [41] here also adds: "and that not of yourselves; it is the gift of God: not of works, lest any man should boast." [42] And lest it should be thought that good works will be wanting in those who believe, he adds further: "For we are His workmanship, created in Christ Jesus unto good works, which God hath before ordained that we should walk in them." [43] We shall be made truly free, then, when God fashions us, that is, forms and creates us anew, not as men—for He has done that already—but as good men, which His grace is now doing, that we may be a new creation in Christ Jesus, according as it is said: "Create in me a clean heart, O God." [44] For God had already created his heart, so far as the physical structure of the human heart is concerned; but the psalmist prays for the renewal of the life which was still lingering in his heart.

[41] 1 Cor. vii. 25
[42] Eph. ii. 8, 9
[43] Eph. ii. 10
[44] Ps. li. 10

XXXII. The Freedom of the Will Is Also the Gift of God, for God Worketh in Us Both to Will and to Do

And further, should any one be inclined to boast, not indeed of his works, but of the freedom of his will, as if the first merit belonged to him, this very liberty of good action being given to him as a reward he had earned, let him listen to this same preacher of grace, when he says: "For it is God which worketh in you, both to will and to do ot His own good pleasure;" [45] and in another place: "So, then, it is not of him that willeth, nor of him that runneth, but of God that showeth mercy." [46] Now as, undoubtedly, if a man is of the age to use his reason, he cannot believe, hope, love, unless he will to do so, nor obtain the prize of the high calling of God unless he voluntarily run for it; in what sense is it "not of him that willeth, nor of him that runneth, but of God that showeth mercy," except that, as it is written, "the preparation of the heart is from the Lord"? [47] Otherwise, if it is said, "It is not of him that willeth, nor of him that runneth, but of God that showeth mercy," because it is of both, that is, both of the will of God, so that we are to understand the saying, "It is not of him that willeth, nor of him that runneth, but of God that showeth mercy," as if

[45] Phil. ii. 13
[46] Rom. ix. 16
[47] Prov. xvi. 1

it meant the will of man alone is not sufficient, if the mercy of God go not with it—then it will follow that the mercy of God alone is not sufficient, if the will of man go not with it; and therefore, if we may rightly say, "it is not of man that willeth, but of God that showeth mercy," because the will of man by itself is not enough, why may we not also rightly put it in the converse way: "It is not of God that showeth mercy, but of man that willeth," because the mercy of God by itself does not suffice? Surely, if no Christian will dare to say this, "It is not of God that showeth mercy, but of man that willeth," lest he should openly contradict the apostle, it follows that the true interpretation of the saying, "It is not of him that willeth, nor of him that runneth, but of God that showeth mercy," is that the whole work belongs to God, who both makes the will of man righteous, and thus prepares it for assistance, and assists it when it is prepared. For the man's righteousness of will precedes many of God's gifts, but not all; and it must itself be included among those which it does not precede. We read in Holy Scripture, both that God's mercy "shall meet me," [48] and that His mercy "shall follow me." [49] It goes before the unwilling to make him willing; it follows the willing to make his will effectual. Why are we taught to pray for our enemies,[50] who are plainly unwilling to lead a holy life, unless that God may work willingness

[48] Ps. lix. 10
[49] Ps. xxiii. 6
[50] Matt. v. 44

in them? And why are we ourselves taught to ask that we may receive,[51] unless that He who has created in us the wish, may Himself satisfy the wish? We pray, then, for our enemies, that the mercy of God may prevent them, as it has prevented us: we pray for ourselves that His mercy may follow us.

XXXIII. Men, Being by Nature the Children of Wrath, Needed a Mediator. In What Sense God Is Said to Be Angry

And so the human race was lying under a just condemnation, and all men were the children of wrath. Of which wrath it is written: "All our days are passed away in Thy wrath; we spend our years as a tale that is told." [52] Of which wrath also Job says: "Man that is born of a woman is of few days, and full of trouble." [53] Of which wrath also the Lord Jesus says: "He that believeth on the Son hath everlasting life: and he that believeth not the Son shall not see life; but the wrath of God abideth on him." [54] He does not say it will come, but it "abideth on him." For every man is born with it; wherefore the apostle says: "We were by nature the children of wrath, even as others." [55] Now, as men were lying under this wrath by reason of their original sin, made the more

[51] Matt. vii. 7
[52] Ps. xc. 9
[53] Job xiv. 1
[54] John iii. 36. These words, attributed by the author to Christ, were really spoken by John the Baptist
[55] Eph. ii. 3

heavy and deadly in proportion to the number
and magnitude of the actual sins which were
added to it, there was need for a Mediator, that
is, for a reconciler, who, by the offering of one
sacrifice, of which all the sacrifices of the law
and the prophets were types, should take away
this wrath. Wherefore the apostle says: "For if,
when we were enemies, we were reconciled to
God by the death of His Son, much more, being
reconciled, we shall be saved by His life." [56]
Now when God is said to be angry, we do not
attribute to Him such a disturbed feeling as
exists in the mind of an angry man; but we
call His just displeasure against sin by the name
"anger," a word transferred by analogy from
human emotions. But our being reconciled to
God through a Mediator, and receiving the
Holy Spirit, so that we who were enemies are
made sons ("For as many as are led by the
Spirit of God, they are the sons of God" [57]):
this is the grace of God through Jesus Christ
our Lord.

XXXIV. THE INEFFABLE MYSTERY OF THE BIRTH OF CHRIST THE MEDIATOR THROUGH THE VIRGIN MARY

Now of this Mediator it would occupy too
much space to say anything at all worthy of
Him; and, indeed, to say what is worthy of
Him is not in the power of man. For who will

[56] Rom. v. 10
[57] Rom. viii. 14

explain in consistent words this single statement, that "the Word was made flesh, and dwelt among us," [58] so that we may believe on the only Son of God the Father Almighty, born of the Holy Spirit and the Virgin Mary? The meaning of the Word being made flesh, is not that the divine nature was changed into flesh, but that the divine nature assumed our flesh. And by "flesh" we are here to understand "man," the part being put for the whole, as when it is said: "By the deeds of the law shall no flesh be justified," [59] that is, no man. For we must believe that no part was wanting in that human nature which He put on, save that it was a nature wholly free from every taint of sin—not such a nature as is conceived between the two sexes through carnal lust, which is born in sin, and whose guilt is washed away in regeneration; but such as it behoved a virgin to bring forth, when the mother's faith, not her lust, was the condition of conception. And if her virginity had been marred even in bringing Him forth, He would not have been born of a virgin; and it would be false (which God forbid) that He was born of the Virgin Mary, as is believed and declared by the whole Church, which, in imitation of His mother, daily brings forth members of His body, and yet remains a virgin. Read, if you please, my letter on the virginity of the holy Mary which I sent to that eminent man, whose name I mention with respect and affection, Volusianus.[60]

[58] John i. 14
[59] Rom. iii. 20
[60] Ep. 137

XXXV. Jesus Christ, Being the Only Son of God, Is at the Same Time Man

Wherefore Christ Jesus, the Son of God, is both God and man; God before all worlds; man in our world: God, because the Word of God (for "the Word was God" [61]); and man, because in His one person the Word was joined with a body and a rational soul. Wherefore, so far as He is God, He and the Father are one; so far as He is man, the Father is greater than He. For when He was the only Son of God, not by grace, but by nature, that He might be also full of grace, He became the Son of man; and He Himself unites both natures in His own identity, and both natures constitute one Christ; because, "being in the form of God, He thought it not robbery to be," what He was by nature, "equal with God." [62] But He made Himself of no reputation, and took upon Himself the form of a servant, not losing or lessening the form of God. And, accordingly, He was both made less and remained equal, being both in one, as has been said: but He was one of these as Word, and the other as man. As Word, He is equal with the Father; as man, less than the Father. One Son of God, and at the same time Son of man; one Son of man, and at the same time Son of God; not two Sons of God, God and man, but one Son of God: God without be-

[61] John i. 1
[62] Phil. ii. 6

ginning; man with a beginning, our Lord Jesus
Christ.

XXXVI. The Grace of God Is Clearly and Remarkably Displayed in Raising the Man Christ Jesus to the Dignity of the Son of God

Now here the grace of God is displayed with
the greatest power and clearness. For what
merit had the human nature in the man Christ
earned, that it should in this unparalleled way
be taken up into the unity of the person of the
only Son of God? What goodness of will, what
goodness of desire and intention, what good
works, had gone before, which made this man
worthy to become one person with God? Had
He been a man previously to this, and had He
earned this unprecedented reward, that He
should be thought worthy to become God?
Assuredly nay; from the very moment that He
began to be man, He was nothing else than the
Son of God, the only Son of God, the Word
who was made flesh, and therefore He was God;
so that just as each individual man unites in
one person a body and a rational soul, so Christ
in one person unites the Word and man. Now
wherefore was this unheard of glory conferred
on human nature—a glory which, as there was
no antecedent merit, was of course wholly of
grace—except that here those who looked at
the matter soberly and honestly might behold a
clear manifestation of the power of God's free
grace, and might understand that they are justi-

fied from their sins by the same grace which made the man Christ Jesus free from the possibility of sin? And so the angel, when he announced to Christ's mother the coming birth, saluted her thus: "Hail, full of grace;" [63] and shortly afterwards, "Thou hast found grace with God." [64] Now she was said to be full of grace, and to have found grace with God, because she was to be the mother of her Lord, nay, of the Lord of all flesh. But, speaking of Christ Himself, the evangelist John, after saying, "The Word was made flesh, and dwelt among us," adds, "and we behold His glory, the glory as of the only-begotten of the Father, full of grace and truth." [65] When he says, "The Word was made flesh," this is "full of grace;" when he says, "the glory of the only-begotten of the Father," this is "full of truth." For the Truth Himself, who was the only-begotten of the Father, not by grace, but by nature, by grace took our humanity upon Him, and so united it with His own person that He Himself became also the Son of man.

XXXVII. The Same Grace Is Further Clearly Manifested in This, That the Birth of Christ According to the Flesh Is of the Holy Spirit

For the same Jesus Christ who is the only-begotten, that is, the only Son of God, our Lord,

[63] Luke i. 28
[64] Luke i. 30
[65] John i. 14

was born of the Holy Spirit and of the Virgin
Mary. And we know that the Holy Spirit is the
gift of God, the gift being Himself indeed equal
to the Giver. And therefore the Holy Spirit also
is God, not inferior to the Father and the Son.
The fact, therefore, that the nativity of Christ
in His human nature was by the Holy Spirit,
is another clear manifestation of grace. For
when the Virgin asked the angel how this which
he had announced should be, seeing she knew
not a man, the angel answered, "The Holy Spirit
shall come upon thee, and the power of the
Highest shall overshadow thee: therefore also
that holy thing which shall be born of thee
shall be called the Son of God." [66] And when
Joseph was minded to put her away, suspecting
her of adultery, as he knew she was not with
child by himself, he was told by the angel,
"Fear not to take unto thee Mary thy wife; for
that which is conceived in her is of the Holy
Spirit:" [67] that is, what thou suspectest to be
begotten of another man is of the Holy Spirit.

XXXVIII. Jesus Christ, According to the Flesh, Was Not Born of the Holy Spirit in Such a Sense That the Holy Spirit Is His Father

Nevertheless, are we on this account to say
that the Holy Spirit is the father of the man
Christ, and that as God the Father begat the
Word, so God the Holy Spirit begat the man,

[66] Luke i. 35
[67] Matt. i. 20

and that these two substances constitute the one
Christ; and that as the Word He is the Son of
God the Father, and as man the Son of God
the Holy Spirit, because the Holy Spirit as His
father begat Him of the Virgin Mary? Who
will dare to say so? Nor is it necessary to show
by reasoning how many other absurdities flow
from this supposition, when it is itself so absurd
that no believer's ears can bear to hear it.
Hence, as we confess, "Our Lord Jesus Christ,
who of God is God, and as man was born of
the Holy Spirit and of the Virgin Mary, having
both substances, the divine and the human, is
the only Son of God the Father Almighty, from
whom proceedeth the Holy Spirit." [68] Now in
what sense do we say that Christ was born of
the Holy Spirit, if the Holy Spirit did not beget
Him? Is it that He made Him, since our Lord
Jesus Christ, though as God "all things were
made by Him," [69] yet as man was Himself
made; as the apostle says, "who was made of
the seed of David according to the flesh"? [70]
But as that created thing which the Virgin conceived and brought forth, though it was united
only to the person of the Son, was made by the
whole Trinity (for the works of the Trinity are
not separable), why should the Holy Spirit
alone be mentioned as having made it? Or is
it that, when one of the Three is mentioned as
the author of any work, the whole Trinity is to
be understood as working? That is true, and

[68] A quotation from a form of the Apostles' Creed
anciently in use in the Latin Church
[69] John i. 3
[70] Rom. i. 3

can be proved by examples. But we need not
dwell longer on this solution. For the puzzle
is, in what sense it is said, "born of the Holy
Spirit," when He is in no sense the Son of the
Holy Spirit? For though God made this world,
it would not be right to say that it is the Son
of God, or that it was born of God; we would
say that it was created, or made, or framed, or
ordered by Him, or whatever form of expression
we can properly use. Here, then, when we make
confession that Christ was born of the Holy
Spirit and of the Virgin Mary, it is difficult to
explain how it is that He is not the Son of the
Holy Spirit and is the Son of the Virgin Mary,
when He was born both of Him and of her.
It is clear beyond a doubt that He was not born
of the Holy Spirit as His father, in the same
sense that He was born of the Virgin as His
mother.

XXXIX. Not Everything That Is Born of Another Is to Be Called a Son of That Other

We need not therefore take for granted, that
whatever is born of a thing is forthwith to be
declared the son of that thing. For, to pass over
the fact that a son is born of a man in a different
sense from that in which a hair or a louse is
born of him, neither of these being a son; to
pass over this, I say, as too mean an illustration
for a subject of so much importance: it is certain
that those who are born of water and of the

Holy Spirit cannot with propriety be called
sons of the water, though they are called sons of
God the Father, and of the Church their mother.
In the same way, then, He who was born of
the Holy Spirit is the Son of God the Father, not
of the Holy Spirit. For what I have said of the
hair and the other things is sufficient to show
us that not everything which is born of another
can be called the son of that of which it is born,
just as it does not follow that all who are called
a man's sons were born of him, for some sons
are adopted. And some men are called sons of
hell, not as being born of hell, but as prepared
for it, as the sons of the kingdom are prepared
for the kingdom.

XL. Christ's Birth Through the Holy Spirit Manifests to Us the Grace of God

And, therefore, as one thing may be born of
another, and yet not in such a way as to be its
son, and as not every one who is called a son
was born of him whose son he is called, it is
clear that this arrangement by which Christ was
born of the Holy Spirit, but not as His son, and
of the Virgin Mary as her son, is intended as a
manifestation of the grace of God. For it was
by this grace that a man, without any antecedent merit, was at the very commencement of
His existence as man, so united in one person
with the Word of God, that the very person who
was Son of man was at the same time Son of

God, and the very person who was Son of God was at the same time Son of man; and in the adoption of His human nature into the divine, the grace itself became in a way so natural to the man, as to leave no room for entrance of sin. Wherefore this grace is signified by the Holy Spirit; for He, though in His own nature God, may also be called the gift of God. And to explain all this sufficiently, if indeed it could be done at all, would require a very lengthened discussion.

XLI. CHRIST, WHO WAS HIMSELF FREE FROM SIN WAS MADE SIN FOR US, THAT WE MIGHT BE RECONCILED TO GOD

Begotten and conceived, then, without any indulgence of carnal lust, and therefore bringing with Him no original sin, and by the grace of God joined and united in a wonderful and unspeakable way in one person with the Word, the Only-begotten of the Father, a son by nature, not by grace, and therefore having no sin of His own; nevertheless, on account of the likeness of sinful flesh in which He came, He was called sin, that He might be sacrificed to wash away sin. For, under the Old Covenant, sacrifices for sin were called sins.[71] And He, of whom all these sacrifices were types and shadows, was Himself truly made sin. Hence the apostle, after saying, "We pray you in Christ's stead, be ye reconciled to God," forthwith adds:

[71] Hos. iv. 8

"for He hath made Him to be sin for us who knew no sin; that we might be made the righteousness of God in Him." [72] He does not say, as some incorrect copies read, "He who knew no sin did sin for us," as if Christ had Himself sinned for our sakes; but he says, "Him who knew no sin," that is, Christ, God, to whom we are to be reconciled, "hath made to be sin for us," that is, hath made Him a sacrifice for our sins, by which we might be reconciled to God. He, then, being made sin, just as we are made righteousness (our righteousness being not our own, but God's, not in ourselves, but in Him); He being made sin, not His own, but ours, not in Himself, but in us, showed, by the likeness of sinful flesh in which He was crucified, that though sin was not in Him, yet that in a certain sense He died to sin, by dying in the flesh which was the likeness of sin; and that although He Himself had never lived the old life of sin, yet by His resurrection He typified our new life springing up out of the old death in sin.

XLII. THE SACRAMENT OF BAPTISM INDICATES OUR DEATH WITH CHRIST TO SIN, AND OUR RESURRECTION WITH HIM TO NEWNESS OF LIFE

And this is the meaning of the great sacrament of baptism which is solemnized among us, that all who attain to this grace should die to sin, as He is said to have died to sin, because

[72] 2 Cor. v. 20, 21

He died in the flesh, which is the likeness of
sin; and rising from the font regenerate, as He
arose alive from the grave, should begin a new
life in the Spirit, whatever may be the age of
the body.

XLIII. Baptism and the Grace Which it Typifies Are Open to All, Both Infants and Adults

For from the infant newly born to the old
man bent with age, as there is none shut out
from baptism, so there is none who in baptism
does not die to sin. But infants die only to
original sin; those who are older die also to
all the sins which their evil lives have added
to the sin which they brought with them.

XLIV. In Speaking of Sin, the Singular Number Is Often Put for the Plural, and the Plural for the Singular

But even these latter are frequently said to
die to sin, though undoubtedly they die not to
one sin, but to all the numerous actual sins they
have committed in thought, word, or deed: for
the singular number is often put for the plural,
as when the poet says, "They fill its belly with
the armed soldier," [73] though in the case here
referred to there were many soldiers concerned.

[73] "Uterumque armato milite complent."—Virgil, *Aen.*
ii. 20

And we read in our own Scriptures: "Pray to the Lord, that He take away the serpent from us." [74] He does not say *serpents*, though the people were suffering from many; and so in other cases. When, on the other hand, the original sin is expressed in the plural number, as when we say that infants are baptized for the remission of *sins*, instead of saying for the remission of *sin*, this is the converse figure of speech, by which the plural number is put in place of the singular; as in the Gospel it is said of the death of Herod, "for they are dead which sought the young child's life," [75] instead of saying, "he is dead." And in *Exodus:* "They have made them," Moses says, "gods of gold," [76] though they had made only one calf, of which they said: "These be thy gods, O Israel, which brought thee up out of the land of Egypt" [77] —here, too, putting the plural in place of the singular.

XLV. In Adam's First Sin, Many Kinds of Sin Were Involved

However, even in that one sin, which "by one man entered into the world, and so passed upon all men," [78] and on account of which infants are baptized, a number of distinct sins may be ob-

[74] Num. xxi. 7
[75] Matt. ii. 20
[76] Ex. xxxii. 31
[77] Ex. xxxii. 4
[78] Rom. v. 12

served, if it be analyzed as it were into its separate elements. For there is in it pride, because man chose to be under his own dominion, rather than under the dominion of God; and blasphemy, because he did not believe God; and murder, for he brought death upon himself; and spiritual fornication, for the purity of the human soul was corrupted by the seducing blandishments of the serpent; and theft, for man turned to his own use the food he had been forbidden to touch; and avarice, for he had a craving for more than should have been sufficient for him; and whatever other sin can be discovered on careful reflection to be involved in this one admitted sin.

XLVI. It Is Probable That Children Are Involved in the Guilt Not Only of the First Pair, but of Their Own Immediate Parents

And it is said, with much appearance of probability, that infants are involved in the guilt of the sins not only of the first pair, but of their own immediate parents. For that divine judgment, "I shall visit the iniquities of the fathers upon the children," [79] certainly applies to them before they come under the new covenant by regeneration. And it was this new covenant that was prophesied of, when it was said by Ezekiel, that the sons should not bear

[79] Ex. xx. 5; Deut. v. 9

the iniquity of the fathers, and that it should
no longer be a proverb in Israel, "The fathers
have eaten sour grapes, and the children's teeth
are set on edge." [80] Here lies the necessity that
each man should be born again, that he might
be freed from the sin in which he was born.
For the sins committed afterwards can be cured
by penitence, as we see is the case after baptism. And therefore the new birth would not
have been appointed only that the first birth
was sinful, so sinful that even one who was
legitimately born in wedlock says: "I was shapen
in iniquities, and in sins did my mother conceive me." [81] He did not say in *iniquity*, or in
sin, though he might have said so correctly; but
he preferred to say "iniquities" and "sins," because in that one sin which passed upon all men,
and which was so great that human nature was
by it made subject to inevitable death, many
sins, as I showed above, may be discriminated;
and further, because there are other sins of the
immediate parents, which, though they have
not the same effect in producing a change of
nature, yet subject the children to guilt unless
the divine grace and mercy interpose to rescue
them.

[80] Ezek. xviii. 2
[81] Ps. li. 5

XLVII. It Is Difficult to Decide Whether the Sins of a Man's Other Progenitors Are Imputed to Him

But about the sins of the other progenitors who intervene between Adam and a man's own parents, a question may very well be raised. Whether every one who is born is involved in all their accumulated evil acts, in all their multiplied original guilt, so that the later he is born, so much the worse is his condition; or whether God threatens to visit the iniquity of the fathers upon the children unto the third and fourth generations because in His mercy He does not extend His wrath against the sins of the progenitors further than that, lest those who do not obtain the grace of regeneration might be crushed down under too heavy a burden if they were compelled to bear as original guilt all the sins of all their progenitors from the very beginning of the human race, and to pay the penalty due to them; or whether any other solution of this great question may or may not be found in Scripture by a more diligent search and a more careful interpretation, I dare not rashly affirm.

XLVIII. The Guilt of the First Sin Is So Great That It Can Be Washed Away Only in the Blood of the Mediator, Jesus Christ

Nevertheless, that one sin, admitted into a place where such perfect happiness reigned, was of so heinous a character, that in one man the whole human race was originally, and as one may say, radically, condemned; and it cannot be pardoned and blotted out except through the one Mediator between God and men, the man Christ Jesus, who only has had power to be so born as not to need a second birth.

XLIX. Christ Was Not Regenerated in the Baptism of John, but Submitted to It to Give Us an Example of Humility, Just as He Submitted to Death, Not as the Punishment of Sin, but to Take Away the Sin of the World

Now, those who were baptized in the baptism of John, by whom Christ was Himeslf baptized,[82] were not regenerated; but they were prepared through the ministry of His forerunner, who cried, "Prepare ye the way of the Lord," [83] for Him in whom only they could be regenerated. For His baptism is not with water

[82] Matt. iii. 13-15
[83] Matt. iii. 3

only, as was that of John, but with the Holy
Spirit also;[84] so that whoever believes in Christ
is regenerated by that Spirit, of whom Christ
being generated, He did not need regeneration.
Whence that announcement of the Father which
was heard after His baptism, "This day have I
begotten Thee," [85] referred not to that one day
of time on which He was baptized, but to the
one day of an unchangeable eternity, so as to
show that this man was one in person with
the Only-begotten. For when a day neither begins with the close of yesterday, nor ends with
the beginning of to-morrow, it is an eternal today. Therefore He asked to be baptized in
water by John, not that any iniquity of His
might be washed away, but that He might
manifest the depth of His humility. For baptism found in Him nothing to wash away, as
death found in Him nothing to punish; so that
it was in the strictest justice, and not by the
mere violence of power, that the devil was
crushed and conquered: for, as he had most
unjustly put Christ to death, though there was
no sin in Him to deserve death, it was most
just that through Christ he should lose his hold
of those who by sin were justly subject to the
bondage in which he held them. Both of these,
then, that is, both baptism and death, were submitted to by Him, not through a pitiable necessity, but of His own free pity for us, and as part
of an arrangement by which, as one man

[84] Matt. iii. 11
[85] Ps. ii. 7; Heb. i. 5, v. 5. It is by a mistake that
Augustine quotes these words as pronounced at our
Lord's baptism

brought sin into the world, that is, upon the whole human race, so one man was to take away the sin of the world.

L. Christ Took Away Not Only the One Original Sin, but All the Other Sins That Have Been Added to It

With this difference: the first man brought one sin into the world, but this man took away not only that one sin, but all that He found added to it. Hence the apostle says: "And not as it was by one that sinned, so is the gift: for the judgment was by one to condemnation, but the free gift is of many offenses unto justification." [86] For it is evident that the one sin which we bring with us by nature would, even if it stood alone, bring us under condemnation; but the free gift justifies man from many offenses: for each man, in addition to the one sin which, in common with all his kind, he brings with him by nature, has committed many sins that are strictly his own.

LI. All Men Born of Adam Are Under Condemnation, and Only if New Born in Christ Are Freed From Condemnation

But what he says a little after, "Therefore, as by the offense of one judgment came upon all

[86] Rom. v. 16

men to condemnation; even so by the righteousness of one the free gift came upon all men unto justification of life," [87] shows clearly enough that there is no one born of Adam but is subject to condemnation, and that no one, unless he be new born in Christ, is freed from condemnation.

LII. In Baptism, Which Is the Similitude of the Death and Resurrection of Christ, All, Both Infants and Adults, Die to Sin That They May Walk in Newness of Life

And after he has said as much about the condemnation through one man, and the free gift through one man, as he deemed sufficient for that part of his epistle, the apostle goes on to speak of the great mystery of holy baptism in the cross of Christ, and to explain clearly to us that baptism in Christ is nothing else than a similitude of the death of Christ, and that the death of Christ on the cross is nothing but a similitude of the pardon of sin: so that just as real as is His death, so real is the remission of our sins; and just as real as is His resurrection, so real is our justification. He says: "What shall we say, then? Shall we continue in sin, that grace may abound?" [88] For he had said previously, "But where sin abounded, grace did

[87] Rom. v. 18
[88] Rom. vi. 1

much more abound." [89] And therefore he pro-
poses to himself the question, whether it would
be right to continue in sin for the sake of the
consequent abounding grace. But he answers,
"God forbid;" and adds, "How shall we, that
are dead to sin, live any longer therein?" Then,
to show that we are dead to sin, "Know ye not,"
he says, "that so many of us as were baptized
into Jesus Christ, were baptized into His death?"
If, then, the fact that we were baptized into the
death of Christ proves that we are dead to sin,
it follows that even infants who are baptized
into Christ die to sin, being baptized into His
death. For there is no exception made: "So
many of us as were baptized into Jesus Christ,
were baptized into His death." And this is said
to prove that we are dead to sin. Now, to what
sin do infants die in their regeneration but that
sin which they bring with them at birth? And
therefore to these also applies what follows:
"Therefore we are buried with Him by baptism
into death; that, like as Christ was raised up
from the dead by the glory of the Father, even
so we also should walk in newness of life. For if
we have been planted together in the likeness
of His death, we shall be also in the likeness of
His resurrection: knowing this, that our old man
is crucified with Him, that the body of sin
might be destroyed, that henceforth we should
not serve sin. For he that is dead is freed from
sin. Now if we be dead with Christ, we believe
that we shall also live with Him: knowing that
Christ, being raised from the dead, dieth no

[89] Rom. v. 20

more; death hath no more dominion over Him. For in that He died, He died unto sin once; but in that He liveth, He liveth unto God. Likewise reckon ye also yourselves to be dead indeed unto sin, but alive unto God through Jesus Christ our Lord." Now he had commenced with proving that we must not continue in sin that grace may abound, and had said: "How shall we that are dead to sin live any longer therein?" And to show that we are dead to sin, he added: "Know ye not, that so many of us as were baptized into Jesus Christ, were baptized into His death?" And so he concludes this whole passage just as he began it. For he has brought in the death of Christ in such a way as to imply that Christ Himself also died to sin. To what sin did He die if not to the flesh, in which there was not sin, but the likeness of sin, and which was therefore called by the name of sin? To those who are baptized into the death of Christ, then—and this class includes not adults only, but infants as well—he says: "Likewise reckon ye also yourselves to be dead indeed unto sin, but alive unto God through Jesus Christ our Lord." [90]

LIII. Christ's Cross and Burial, Resurrection, Ascension, and Sitting Down at the Right Hand of God, Are Images of the Christian Life

All the events, then, of Christ's crucifixion, of His burial, of His resurrection the third day, of

[90] Rom. vi. 1-11

His ascension into heaven, of His sitting down at the right hand of the Father, were so ordered, that the life which the Christian leads here might be modelled upon them, not merely in a mystical sense, but in reality. For in reference to His crucifixion it is said: "They that are Christ's have crucified the flesh, with the affections and lusts." [91] And in reference to His burial: "We are buried with Him by baptism into death." [92] In reference to His resurrection: "That, like as Christ was raised up from the dead by the glory of the Father, even so we also should walk in newness of life." [93] And in reference to His ascension into heaven and sitting down at the right hand of the Father: "If ye then be risen with Christ, seek those things which are above, where Christ sitteth on the right hand of God. Set your affection on things above, not on things on the earth. For ye are dead, and your life is hid with Christ in God." [94]

LIV. Christ's Second Coming Does Not Belong to the Past, but Will Take Place at the End of the World

But what we believe as to Christ's action in the future, when He shall come from heaven to judge the quick and the dead, has no bearing

[91] Gal. v. 24
[92] Rom. vi. 4
[93] Rom. vi. 5
[94] Col. iii. 1-3

upon the life which we now lead here; for it forms no part of what He did upon earth, but is part of what He shall do at the end of the world. And it is to this that the apostle refers in what immediately follows the passage quoted above: "When Christ, who is your life shall appear, then shall ye also appear with Him in glory." [95]

LV. The Expression, "Christ Shall Judge the Quick and the Dead," May Be Understood in Either of Two Senses

Now the expression, "to judge the quick and the dead," may be interpreted in two ways: either we may understand by the "quick" those who at His advent shall not yet have died, but whom He shall find alive in the flesh, and by the "dead" those who have departed from the body, or who shall have departed before His coming; or we may understand the "quick" to mean the righteous, and the "dead" the unrighteous; for the righteous shall be judged as well as others. Now the judgment of God is sometimes taken in a bad sense, as, for example, "They that have done evil unto the resurrection of judgment;" [96] sometimes in a good sense, as, "Save me, O God, by Thy name, and judge me by Thy strength." [97] This is easily understood

[95] Col. iii. 4
[96] John v. 29
[97] Ps. liv. 1

when we consider that it is the judgment of
God which separates the good from the evil,
and sets the good at His right hand, that they
may be delivered from evil, and not destroyed
with the wicked; and it is for this reason that
the Psalmist cried, "Judge me, O God," and
then added, as if in explanation, "and distinguish
my cause from that of an ungodly nation." [98]

LVI. The Holy Spirit and the Church. The Church Is the Temple of God

And now, having spoken of Jesus Christ, the
only Son of God, our Lord, with the brevity
suitable to a confession of our faith, we go on
to say that we believe also in the Holy Spirit—
thus completing the Trinity which constitutes
the Godhead. Then we mention the Holy
Church. And thus we are made to understand
that the intelligent creation, which constitutes
the free Jerusalem,[99] ought to be subordinate in
the order of speech to the Creator, the Supreme
Trinity: for all that is said of the man Christ
Jesus has reference, of course, to the unity of
the person of the Only-begotten. Therefore the
true order of the Creed demanded that the
Church should be made subordinate to the
Trinity, as the house to Him who dwells in it,
the temple to God who occupies it, and the city
to its builder. And we are here to understand
the whole Church, not that part of it only

[98] Ps. xliii. 1
[99] Gal. iv. 26

which wanders as a stranger on the earth, praising the name of God from the rising of the sun to the going down of the same, and singing a new song of deliverance from its old captivity; but that part also which has always from its creation remained steadfast to God in heaven, and has never experienced the misery consequent upon a fall. This part is made up of the holy angels, who enjoy uninterrupted happiness; and (as it is bound to do) it renders assistance to the part which is still wandering among strangers: for these two parts shall be one in the fellowship of eternity, and now they are one in the bonds of love, the whole having been ordained for the worship of the one God. Wherefore, neither the whole Church, nor any part of it, has any desire to be worshipped instead of God, nor to be God to any one who belongs to the temple of God—that temple which is built up of the saints who were created by the uncreated God. And therefore the Holy Spirit, if a creature, could not be the Creator, but would be a part of the intelligent creation. He would simply be the highest creature, and therefore would not be mentioned in the Creed before the Church; for He Himself would belong to the Church, to that part of it which is in the heavens. And He would not have a temple, for He Himself would be part of a temple. Now He has a temple, of which the apostle says: "Know ye not that your body is the temple of the Holy Spirit, which is in you, which ye have of God?" [100] Of which body he says in another

[100] 1 Cor. vi. 19

place: "Know ye not that your bodies are the members of Christ?" [101] How, then, is He not God, seeing that He has a temple? and how can He be less than Christ, whose members are His temple? Nor has He one temple, and God another, seeing that the same apostle says: "Know ye not that ye are the temple of God?" [102] and adds, as proof of this, "and that the Spirit of God dwelleth in you"? [103] God, then, dwells in His temple: not the Holy Spirit only, but the Father also, and the Son, who says of His own body, through which He was made Head of the Church upon earth ("that in all things He might have the pre-eminence"):[104] "Destroy this temple, and in three days I will raise it up." [105] The temple of God, then, that is, of the Supreme Trinity as a whole, is the Holy Church, embracing in its full extent both heaven and earth.

LVII. The Condition of the Church in Heaven

But of that part which is in heaven what can we say, except that no wicked one is found in it, and that no one has fallen from it, or shall ever fall from it, since the time that "God spared not the angels that sinned," as the Apostle Peter writes, "but cast them down to hell, and

[101] 1 Cor. vi. 15
[102] 1 Cor. iii. 16
[103] 1 Cor. iii. 16
[104] Col. i. 18
[105] John ii. 19

delivered them into chains of darkness, to be reserved unto judgment"? [106]

LVIII. WE HAVE NO CERTAIN KNOWLEDGE OF THE ORGANIZATION OF THE ANGELIC SOCIETY

Now, what the organization is of that supremely happy society in heaven: what the differences of rank are, which explain the fact that while all are called by the general name *angels*, as we read in the *Epistle to the Hebrews*, "but to which of the angels said God at any time, Sit on my right hand?" [107] (this form of expression being evidently designed to embrace all the angels without exception) we yet find that there are some called *archangels;* and whether the archangels are the same as those called *hosts,* so that the expression, "Praise ye Him, all His angels: praise ye Him, all His hosts," [108] is the same as if it had been said, "Praise ye Him, all His angels: praise ye Him, all His archangels;" and what are the various significations of those four names under which the apostle seems to embrace the whole heavenly company without exception, "whether they be thrones, or dominions, or principalities, or powers:" [109]—let those who are able answer these questions, if they can also prove their answers to be true; but as for me, I confess my

[106] 2 Pet. ii. 4
[107] Heb. i. 13
[108] Ps. cxlviii. 2
[109] Col. i. 16

ignorance. I am not even certain upon this point: whether the sun, and the moon, and all the stars, do not form part of this same society, though many consider them merely luminous bodies, without either sensation or intelligence.

LIX. The Bodies Assumed by Angels Raise a Very Difficult, and Not Very Useful, Subject of Discussion

Further, who will tell with what sort of bodies it was that the angels appeared to men, making themselves not only visible, but tangible; and again, how it is that, not through material bodies, but by spiritual power, they present visions not to the bodily eyes, but to the spiritual eyes of the mind, or speak something not into the ear from without, but from within the soul of the man, they themselves being stationed there too, as it is written in the prophet, "And the angel that spake in me said unto me" [110] (he does not say, "that spake *to* me," but "that spake *in* me"); or appear to men in sleep, and make communications through dreams, as we read in the Gospel, "Behold, the angel of the Lord appeared unto him in a dream, saying"? [111] For these methods of communication seem to imply that the angels have not tangible bodies, and make it a very difficult question to solve how the patriarchs washed their feet,[112] and

[110] Zech. i. 9
[111] Matt. i. 20
[112] Gen. xviii. 4, xix. 2

how it was that Jacob wrestled with the angel
in a way so unmistakeably material.[113] To ask
questions like these, and to make such guesses
as we can at the answers, is a useful exercise
for the intellect, if the discussion be kept within
proper bounds, and if we avoid the error of
supposing ourselves to know what we do not
know. For what is the necessity for affirming, or
denying, or defining with accuracy on these
subjects, and others like them, when we may
without blame be entirely ignorant of them?

LX. It Is More Necessary to Be Able to Detect the Wiles of Satan When He Transforms Himself Into an Angel of Light

It is more necessary to use all our powers of
discrimination and judgment when Satan trans-
forms himself into an angel of light,[114] lest by
his wiles he should lead us astray into hurtful
courses. For, while he only deceives the bodily
senses, and does not pervert the mind from that
true and sound judgment which enables a man
to lead a life of faith, there is no danger to
religion; or if, feigning himself to be good, he
does or says the things that befit good angels,
and we believe him to be good, the error is not
one that is hurtful or dangerous to Christian
faith. But when, through these means, which are
alien to his nature, he goes on to lead us into

[113] Gen. xxxii. 24, 25
[114] 2 Cor. xi. 14

courses of his own, then great watchfulness is
necessary to detect, and refuse to follow, him.
But how many men are fit to evade all his
deadly wiles, unless God restrains and watches
over them? The very difficulty of the matter,
however, is useful in this respect, that it prevents
men from trusting in themselves or in one another, and leads all to place their confidence in
God alone. And certainly no pious man can
doubt that this is most expedient for us.

LXI. The Church on Earth Has Been Redeemed From Sin by the Blood of a Mediator

This part of the Church, then, which is made
up of the holy angels and the hosts of God, shall
become known to us in its true nature, when, at
the end of the world, we shall be united with
it in the common possession of everlasting happiness. But the other part, which, separated
from it, wanders as a stranger on the earth, is
better known to us, both because we belong to
it, and because it is composed of men, and we
too are men. This part has been redeemed from
all sin by the blood of a Mediator who had no
sin, and its song is: "If God be for us, who can
be against us? He that spared not His own Son,
but delivered Him up for us all." [115] Now it was
not for the angels that Christ died. Yet what
was done for the redemption of man through
His death was in a sense done for the angels,

[115] Rom. viii. 31

because the enmity which sin had put between men and the holy angels is removed, and friendship is restored between them, and by the redemption of man the gaps which the great apostasy left in the angelic host are filled up.

LXII. By the Sacrifice of Christ All Things Are Restored, and Peace Is Made Between Earth and Heaven

And, of course, the holy angels, taught by God, in the eternal contemplation of whose truth their happiness consists, know how great a number of the human race are to supplement their ranks, and fill up the full count of their citizenship. Wherefore the apostle says, that "all things are gathered together in one in Christ, both which are in heaven and which are on earth." [116] The things which are in heaven are gathered together when what was lost therefrom in the fall of the angels is restored from among men; and the things which are on earth are gathered together, when those who are predestined to eternal life are redeemed from their old corruption. And thus, through that single sacrifice in which the Mediator was offered up, the one sacrifice of which the many victims under the law were types, heavenly things are brought into peace with earthly things, and earthly things with heavenly. Wherefore, as the same apostle says: "For it pleased the Father that in Him should all fullness dwell:

[116] Eph. i. 10

and, having made peace through the blood of
His cross, by Him to reconcile all things to
Himself: by Him, I say, whether they be things
in earth, or things in heaven." [117]

LXIII. The Peace of God, Which Reigneth in Heaven, Passeth All Understanding

This peace, as Scripture saith, "passeth all
understanding," [118] and cannot be known by us
until we have come into the full possession of
it. For in what sense are heavenly things reconciled, except they be reconciled to us, *viz.* by
coming into harmony with us? For in heaven
there is unbroken peace, both between all the
intelligent creatures that exist there, and between these and their Creator. And this peace,
as is said, passeth all understanding; but this,
of course, means our understanding, not that
of those who always behold the face of their
Father. We now, however great may be our
human understanding, know but in part, and
see through a glass darkly.[119] But when we
shall be equal unto the angels of God [120] then
we shall see face to face, as they do; and we
shall have as great peace towards them as they
have towards us, because we shall love them as
much as we are loved by them. And so their
peace shall be known to us: for our own peace
shall be like to theirs, and as great as theirs,

[117] Col. i. 19, 20
[118] Phil. iv. 7
[119] 1 Cor. xiii. 12
[120] Luke xx. 36

nor shall it then pass our understanding. But the peace of God, the peace which He cherisheth towards us, shall undoubtedly pass not our understanding only, but theirs as well. And this must be so: for every rational creature which is happy derives its happiness from Him; He does not derive His from it. And in this view it is better to interpret "all" in the passage, "The peace of God passeth all understanding," as admitting of no exception even in favor of the understanding of the holy angels: the only exception that can be made is that of God Himself. For, of course, His peace does not pass His own understanding.

LXIV. Pardon of Sin Extends Over the Whole Mortal Life of the Saints, Which, Though Free From Crime, Is Not Free From Sin

But the angels even now are at peace with us when our sins are pardoned. Hence, in the order of the Creed, after the mention of the Holy Church is placed the remission of sins. For it is by this that the Church on earth stands: it is through this that what had been lost, and was found, is saved from being lost again. For, setting aside the grace of baptism, which is given as an antidote to original sin, so that what our birth imposes upon us, our new birth relieves us from (this grace, however, takes away all the actual sins also that have been committed in thought, word, and deed): setting aside, then, this great act of favor, whence commences man's restoration, and in which all our guilt, both original and actual, is washed away, the rest of our life from the time that we have the use of reason provides constant occasion for the remission of sins, however great may be our advance in righteousness. For the sons of God, as long as they live in this body of death, are in conflict with death. And although it is truly said of them, "As many as are led by the Spirit of God, they are the sons of God," [121] yet they are led by the Spirit of God, and as the sons of God advance towards God under this drawback, that they are led also by their own spirit, weighted as it is by the corruptible body;[122] and that, as the sons of men, under the influence of human affections, they fall back to their old level, and so sin. There is a difference, however. For although every crime is a sin, every sin is not a crime. And so we say that the life of holy men, as long as they remain in this mortal body, may be found without crime; but, as the Apostle John says, "If we say that we have no sin, we deceive ourselves, and the truth is not in us." [123]

LXV. God Pardons Sins, but on Condition of Penitence, Certain Times for Which Have Been Fixed by the Law of the Church

But even crimes themselves, however great, may be remitted in the Holy Church; and the

[121] Rom. viii. 14
[122] Wisd. ix. 15
[123] 1 John i. 8

mercy of God is never to be despaired of by men who truly repent, each according to the measure of his sin. And in the act of repentance, where a crime has been committed of such a nature as to cut off the sinner from the body of Christ we are not to take account so much of the measure of time as of the measure of sorrow; for a broken and a contrite heart God doth not despise.[124] But as the grief of one heart is frequently hid from another, and is not made known to others by words or other signs, when it is manifest to Him of whom it is said, "My groaning is not hid from Thee," [125] those who govern the Church have rightly appointed times of penitence, that the Church in which the sins are remitted may be satisfied; and outside the Church sins are not remitted. For the Church alone has received the pledge of the Holy Spirit, without which there is no remission of sins—such, at least, as brings the pardoned to eternal life.

LXVI. The Pardon of Sin Has Reference Chiefly to the Future Judgment

Now the pardon of sin has reference chiefly to the future judgment. For, as far as this life is concerned, the saying of Scripture holds good: "A heavy yoke is upon the sons of Adam, from the day that they go out of their mother's womb, till the day that they return to the mother of

[124] Ps. li. 17
[125] Ps. xxxviii. 9

all things." [126] So that we see even infants, after
baptism and regeneration, suffering from the
infliction of divers evils: and thus we are given
to understand, that all that is set forth in the
sacraments of salvation refers rather to the hope
of future good, than to the retaining or attaining
of present blessings. For many sins seem in this
world to be overlooked and visited with no
punishment, whose punishment is reserved for
the future (for it is not in vain that the day
when Christ shall come as Judge of quick and
dead is peculiarly named the day of judgment);
just as, on the other hand, many sins are
punished in this life, which nevertheless are
pardoned, and shall bring down no punishment
in the future life. Accordingly, in reference to
certain temporal punishments, which in this life
are visited upon sinners, the apostle, addressing
those whose sins are blotted out, and not reserved for the final judgment, says: "For if we
would judge ourselves, we should not be judged.
But when we are judged, we are chastened of
the Lord, that we should not be condemned
with the world." [127]

LXVII. Faith Without Works Is Dead, and Cannot Save a Man

It is believed, moreover, by some, that men
who do not abandon the name of Christ, and
who have been baptized in the Church by His

[126] Ecclus. xl. 1
[127] 1 Cor. xi. 31, 32

baptism, and who have never been cut off from the Church by any schism or heresy, though they should live in the grossest sin, and never either wash it away in penitence nor redeem it by almsgiving, but persevere in it persistently to the last day of their lives, shall be saved by fire: that is, that although they shall suffer a punishment by fire, lasting for a time proportionate to the magnitude of their crimes and misdeeds, they shall not be punished with everlasting fire. But those who believe this, and yet are Catholics, seem to me to be led astray by a kind of benevolent feeling natural to humanity. For Holy Scripture, when consulted, gives a very different answer. I have written a book on this subject, entitled *Of Faith and Works*, in which, to the best of my ability, God assisting me, I have shown from Scripture, that the faith which saves us is that which the Apostle Paul clearly enough describes when he says: "For in Jesus Christ neither circumcision availeth anything, nor uncircumcision, but faith which worketh by love." [128] But if it worketh evil, and not good, then without doubt, as the Apostle James says, "it is dead in itself." [129] The same apostle says again, "What doth it profit, my brethren, though a man say he hath faith, and have not works? Can faith save him?" [130] And further, if a wicked man shall be saved by fire on account of his faith alone, and if this is what the blessed Apostle Paul means when he says,

[128] Gal. v. 6
[129] Jas. ii. 17
[130] Jas. ii. 14

"But he himself shall be saved, yet so as by fire;" [131] then faith without works *can* save a man, and what his fellow-apostle James says must be false. And that must be false which Paul himself says in another place: "Be not deceived: neither fornicators, nor idolaters, nor adulterers, nor effeminate, nor abusers of themselves with mankind, nor thieves, nor covetous, nor drunkards, nor revilers, nor extortioners, shall inherit the kingdom of God." [132] For if those who persevere in these wicked courses shall nevertheless be saved on account of their faith in Christ, how can it be true that they shall not inherit the kingdom of God?

LXVIII. The True Sense of the Passage (1 Cor. iii. 11-15) About Those Who Are Saved, Yet So as by Fire

But as these most plain and unmistakable declarations of the apostles cannot be false, that obscure saying about those who build upon the foundation, Christ, not gold, silver, and precious stones, but wood, hay, and stubble (for it is these who, it is said, shall be saved, yet so as by fire, the merit of the foundation saving them[133]), must be so interpreted as not to conflict with the plain statements quoted above. Now wood, hay, and stubble may, without incongruity, be understood to signify such an attachment to worldly things, however lawful

---

[131] 1 Cor. iii. 15
[132] 1 Cor. vi. 9, 10
[133] 1 Cor. iii. 11-15

these may be in themselves, that they cannot be lost without grief of mind. And though this grief burns, yet if Christ hold the place of foundation in the heart—that is, if nothing be preferred to Him, and if the man, though burning with grief, is yet more willing to lose the things he loves so much than to lose Christ—he is saved by fire. If, however, in time of temptation, he prefer to hold by temporal and earthly things rather than by Christ, he has not Christ as his foundation; for he puts earthly things in the first place, and in a building nothing comes before the foundation. Again, the fire of which the apostle speaks in this place must be such a fire as both men are made to pass through, that is, both the man who builds upon the foundation, gold, silver, precious stones, and the man who builds wood, hay, stubble. For he immediately adds: "The fire shall try every man's work, of what sort it is. If any man's work abide which he hath built thereupon, he shall receive a reward. If any man's work shall be burned, he shall suffer loss; but he himself shall be saved, yet so as by fire." [134] The fire then shall prove, not the work of one of them only, but of both. Now the trial of adversity is a kind of fire which is plainly spoken of in another place: "The furnace proveth the potter's vessels: and the furnace of adversity just men." [135] And this fire does in the course of this life act exactly in the way the apostle says. If it come into contact with two believers, one "caring for the things

[134] 1 Cor. iii. 13-15
[135] Ecclus. xxvii. 5, ii. 5

that belong to the Lord, how he may please the
Lord," [136] that is, building upon Christ the foundation, gold, silver, precious stones; the other
"caring for the things that are of the world, how
he may please his wife," that is, building upon
the same foundation wood, hay, stubble—the
work of the former is not burned, because he
has not given his love to things whose loss can
cause him grief; but the work of the latter is
burned, because things that are enjoyed with
desire cannot be lost without pain. But since,
by our supposition, even the latter prefers to
lose these things rather than to lose Christ,
and since he does not desert Christ out of fear
of losing them, though he is grieved when he
does lose them, he is saved, but it is so as by
fire; because the grief for what he loved and has
lost burns him. But it does not subvert nor
consume him; for he is protected by his im-
movable and incorruptible foundation.

LXIX. It Is Not Impossible That Some Believers May Pass Through a Purgatorial Fire in the Future Life

And it is not impossible that something of the
same kind may take place even after this life.
It is a matter that may be inquired into, and
either ascertained or left doubtful, whether
some believers shall pass through a kind of pur-
gatorial fire, and in proportion as they have
loved with more or less devotion the goods that

[136] 1 Cor. vii. 32

perish, be less or more quickly delivered from
it. This cannot, however, be the case of any of
those of whom it is said, that they "shall not
inherit the kingdom of God,"[137] unless after suitable repentance their sins be forgiven them.
When I say "suitable," I mean that they are
not to be unfruitful in almsgiving; for Holy
Scripture lays so much stress on this virtue,
that our Lord tells us beforehand, that He will
ascribe no merit to those on His right hand but
that they abound in it, and no defect to those
on His left hand but their want of it, when He
shall say to the former, "Come, ye blessed of my
Father, inherit the kingdom," and to the latter,
"Depart from me, ye cursed, into everlasting
fire." [138]

LXX. Almsgiving Will Not Atone for Sin Unless the Life Be Changed

We must beware, however, lest any one
should suppose that gross sins, such as are committed by those who shall not inherit the kingdom of God, may be daily perpetrated, and
daily atoned for by almsgiving. The life must be
changed for the better; and almsgiving must be
used to propitiate God for past sins, not to purchase impunity for the commission of such sins
in the future. For He has given no man license
to sin,[139] although in His mercy He may blot

[137] 1 Cor. vi. 10
[138] Matt. xxv. 31-46
[139] Ecclus. xv. 20

out sins that are already committed, if we do not neglect to make proper satisfaction.

LXXI. The Daily Prayer of the Believer Makes Satisfaction for the Trivial Sins That Daily Stain His Life

Now the daily prayer of the believer makes satisfaction for those daily sins of a momentary and trivial kind which are necessary incidents of this life. For he can say, "Our Father which art in heaven," [140] seeing that to such a Father he is now born again of water and of the Spirit.[141] And this prayer certainly takes away the very small sins of daily life. It takes away also those which at one time made the life of the believer very wicked, but which, now that he is changed for the better by repentance, he has given up, provided that as truly as he says, "Forgive us our debts" (for there is no want of debts to be forgiven), so truly does he say, "as we forgive our debtors;" [142] that is, provided he does what he says he does: for to forgive a man who asks for pardon, is really to give alms.

LXXII. There Are Many Kinds of Alms, the Giving of Which Assists to Procure Pardon for Our Sins

And on this principle of interpretation, our Lord's saying, "Give alms of such things as ye

[140] Matt. vi. 9
[141] John iii. 5
[142] Matt. vi. 12

have, and, behold, all things are clean unto you," [143] applies to every useful act that a man does in mercy. Not only, then, the man who gives food to the hungry, drink to the thirsty, clothing to the naked, hospitality to the stranger, shelter to the fugitive, who visits the sick and the imprisoned, ransoms the captive, assists the weak, leads the blind, comforts the sorrowful, heals the sick, puts the wanderer on the right path, gives advice to the perplexed, and supplies the wants of the needy—not this man only, but the man who pardons the sinner also gives alms; and the man who corrects with blows, or restrains by any kind of discipline one over whom he has power, and who at the same time forgives from the heart the sin by which he was injured, or prays that it may be forgiven, is also a giver of alms, not only in that he forgives, or prays for forgiveness for the sin, but also in that he rebukes and corrects the sinner: for in this, too, he shows mercy. Now much good is bestowed upon unwilling recipients, when their advantage and not their pleasure is consulted; and they themselves frequently prove to be their own enemies, while their true friends are those whom they take for their enemies, and to whom in their blindness they return evil for good. (A Christian, indeed, is not permitted to return evil even for evil.[144]) And thus there are many kinds of alms, by giving of which we assist to procure the pardon of our sins.

[143] Luke xi. 41
[144] Rom. xii. 17; Matt. v. 44

LXXIII. The Greatest of All Alms Is to Forgive Our Debtors and to Love Our Enemies

But none of those is greater than to forgive from the heart a sin that has been committed against us. For it is a comparatively small thing to wish well to, or even to do good to, a man who has done no evil to you. It is a much higher thing, and is the result of the most exalted goodness, to love your enemy, and always to wish well to, and when you have the opportunity, to do good to, the man who wishes you ill, and, when he can, does you harm. This is to obey the command of God: "Love your enemies, do good to them that hate you, and pray for them which persecute you." [145] But seeing that this is a frame of mind only reached by the perfect sons of God, and that though every believer ought to strive after it, and by prayer to God and earnest struggling with himself endeavor to bring his soul up to this standard, yet a degree of goodness so high can hardly belong to so great a multitude as we believe are heard when they use this petition, "Forgive us our debts, as we forgive our debtors;" in view of all this, it cannot be doubted that the implied undertaking is fulfilled if a man, though he has not yet attained to loving his enemy, yet, when asked by one who has sinned against him to

[145] Matt. v. 44

forgive his sin, does forgive him from his heart. For he certainly desires to be himself forgiven when he prays, "as we forgive our debtors," that is, Forgive us our debts when we beg forgiveness, as we forgive our debtors when they beg forgiveness from us.

LXXIV. GOD DOES NOT PARDON THE SINS OF THOSE WHO DO NOT FROM THE HEART FORGIVE OTHERS

Now, he who asks forgiveness of the man against whom he has sinned, being moved by his sin to ask forgiveness, cannot be counted an enemy in such a sense that it should be as difficult to love him now as it was when he was engaged in active hostility. And the man who does not from his heart forgive him who repents of his sin, and asks forgiveness, need not suppose that his own sins are forgiven of God. For the Truth cannot lie. And what reader or hearer of the Gospel can have failed to notice, that the same person who said, "I am the Truth,"[146] taught us also this form of prayer; and in order to impress this particular petition deeply upon our minds, said, "For if ye forgive men their trespasses, your heavenly Father will also forgive you; but if ye forgive not men their trespasses, neither will your Father forgive your trespasses"? [147] The man whom the thunder of this warning does not awaken is not asleep, but

[146] John xiv. 6
[147] Matt. vi. 14, 15

dead; and yet so powerful is that voice, that
it can awaken even the dead.

LXXV. The Wicked and the Unbelieving Are Not Made Clean by the Giving of Alms, Except They Be Born Again

Assuredly, then, those who live in gross wickedness, and take no care to reform their lives
and manners, and yet amid all their crimes and
vices do not cease to give frequent alms, in
vain take comfort to themselves from the saying
of our Lord: "Give alms of such things as ye
have; and, behold, all things are clean unto
you." [148] For they do not understand how far
this saying reaches. But that they may understand this, let them note to whom He said it.
For we read in the Gospel as follows: "And as
He spake, a certain Pharisee besought Him to
dine with him; and He went in, and sat down
to meat. And when the Pharisee saw it, he
marvelled that He had not first washed before
dinner. And the Lord said unto him, Now do
ye Pharisees make clean the outside of the cup
and the platter; but your inward part is full of
ravening and wickedness. Ye fools, did not he
that made that which is without, make that
which is within also? But rather give alms of
such things as ye have; and, behold, all things
are clean unto you." [149] Are we to understand
this as meaning that to the Pharisees who have

[148] Luke xi. 41
[149] Luke xi. 37-41

not the faith of Christ all things are clean, if only they give alms in the way these men count almsgiving, even though they have never believed in Christ, nor been born again of water and of the Spirit? But the fact is, that all are unclean who are not made clean by the faith of Christ, according to the expression, "purifying their hearts by faith;" [150] and that the apostle says, "Unto them that are defiled and unbelieving is nothing pure; but even their mind and conscience is defiled." [151] How, then, could all things be clean to the Pharisees, even though they gave alms, if they were not believers? And how could they be believers if they were not willing to have faith in Christ, and to be born again of His grace? And yet what they heard is true: "Give alms of such things as ye have; and, behold, all things are clean unto you."

LXXVI. To Give Alms Aright, We Should Begin With Ourselves, and Have Pity Upon Our Own Souls

For the man who wishes to give alms as he ought, should begin with hmiself, and give to himself first. For almsgiving is a work of mercy; and most truly is it said, "To have mercy on thy soul is pleasing to God." [152] And for this end are we born again, that we should be pleasing to God, who is justly displeased with that which

[150] Acts xv. 9
[151] Tit. i. 15
[152] Ecclus. xxx. 24

we brought with us when we were born. This
is our first alms, which we give to ourselves
when, through the mercy of a pitying God, we
find that we are ourselves wretched, and confess
the justice of His judgment by which we are
made wretched, of which the apostle says, "The
judgment was by one to condemnation;" [153]
and praise the greatness of His love, of which
the same preacher of grace says, "God com-
mendeth His love toward us, in that, while we
were yet sinners, Christ died for us:" [154] and
thus, judging truly of our own misery, and
loving God with the love which He has Himself
bestowed, we lead a holy and virtuous life. But
the Pharisees, while they gave as alms the tithe
of all their fruits, even the most insignificant,
passed over the judgment and the love of God,
and so did not commence their almsgiving at
home, and extend their pity to themselves in the
first instance. And it is in reference to this order
of love that it is said, "Love thy neighbor as
thyself." [155] When, then, our Lord had rebuked
them because they made themselves clean on
the outside, but within were full of ravening
and wickedness, He advised them, in the exercise of that charity which each man owes to
himself in the first instance, to make clean the
inward parts. "But rather," He says, "give alms
of such things as ye have; and, behold, all things
are clean unto you." [156] Then, to show what it
was that He advised, and what they took no

[153] Rom. v. 16
[154] Rom. v. 8
[155] Luke x. 27
[156] Luke xi. 41.

pains to do, and to show that He did not over-
look or forget their almsgiving, "But woe unto
you, Pharisees!" He says; as if He meant to
say: I indeed advise you to give alms which
shall make all things clean unto you; "but woe
unto you! for ye tithe mint, and rue, and all
manner of herbs;" as if He meant to say: I know
these alms of yours, and ye need not think that
I am now admonishing you in respect of such
things; "and pass over judgment and the love of
God," and alms by which ye might have been
made clean from all inward impurity, so that
even the bodies which ye are now washing
would have been clean to you. For this is the
import of "all things," both inward and outward
things, as we read in another place: "Cleanse
first that which is within, that the outside may
be clean also." [157] But lest He might appear to
despise the alms which they were giving out of
the fruits of the earth, He says: "These ought
ye to have done," referring to the judgment and
the love of God, "and not to leave the other
undone," referring to the giving of the tithes.

LXXVII. If We Would Give Alms to Ourselves, We Must Flee Iniquity, for He
Who Loveth Iniquity Hateth His Soul

Those, then, who think that they can by giving
alms, however profuse, whether in money or
in kind, purchase for themselves the privilege
of persisting with impunity in their monstrous

[157] Matt. xxiii. 26

crimes and hideous vices, need not thus deceive
themselves. For not only do they commit these
sins, but they love them so much that they
would like to go on forever committing them,
if only they could do so with impunity. Now,
he who loveth iniquity hateth his own soul;[158]
and he who hateth his own soul is not merciful
but cruel towards it. For in loving it according
to the world, he hateth it according to God.
But if he desired to give alms to it which should
make all things clean unto him, he would hate
it according to the world, and love it according
to God. Now no one gives alms unless he receive
what he gives from one who is not in want of
it. Therefore it is said, "His mercy shall meet
me." [159]

LXXVIII. What Sins Are Trivial and What Heinous Is a Matter For God's Judgment

Now, what sins are trivial and what heinous
is not a matter to be decided by man's judgment,
but by the judgment of God. For it is plain
that the apostles themselves have given an
indulgence in the case of certain sins: take, for
example, what the Apostle Paul says to those
who are married: "Defraud ye not one the other,
except it be with consent for a time, that ye may
give yourselves to fasting and prayer: and come

[158] Ps. xi. 5
[159] Ps. lix. 10

together again, that Satan tempt you not for
your incontinency." [160] Now it is possible that
it might not have been considered a sin to have
intercourse with a spouse, not with a view to the
procreation of children, which is the great blessing of marriage, but for the sake of carnal
pleasure, and to save the incontinent from being
led by their weakness into the deadly sin of
fornication, or adultery, or another form of un-
cleanness which it is shameful even to name,
and into which it is possible that they might be
drawn by lust under the temptation of Satan.
It is possible, I say, that this might not have been
considered a sin, had the apostle not added.
"But I speak this by permission, and not of commandment." [161] Who, then, can deny that it is
a sin, when confessedly it is only by apostolic
authority that permission is granted to those
who do it? Another case of the same kind is
where he says: "Dare any of you, having a
matter against another, go to law before the
unjust and not before the saints?" [162] And shortly
afterwards: "If then ye have judgments of things
pertaining to this life, set them to judge who
are least esteemed in the Church. I speak to
your shame. Is it so, that there is not a wise
man among you? no, not one that shall be able
to judge between his brethren? But brother
goeth to law with brother, and that before the
unbelievers." [163] Now it might have been sup-

[160] 1 Cor. vii. 5
[161] 1 Cor. vii. 6
[162] 1 Cor. vi. 1
[163] 1 Cor. vi. 4-6

posed in this case that it is not a sin to have a
quarrel with another, that the only sin is in
wishing to have it adjudicated upon outside the
Church, had not the apostle immediately added:
"Now therefore there is utterly a fault among
you, because ye go to law with one another." [164]
And lest any one should excuse himself by saying that he had a just cause, and was suffering
wrong, and that he only wished the sentence
of the judges to remove his wrong, the apostle
immediately anticipates such thoughts and ex-
cuses, and says: "Why do ye not rather take
wrong? Why do ye not rather suffer yourselves
to be defrauded?" Thus bringing us back to
our Lord's saying, "If any man will sue thee at
the law, and take away thy coat, let him have
thy cloak also;" [165] and again, "Of him that
taketh away thy goods, ask them not again." [166]
Therefore our Lord has forbidden His followers
to go to law with other men about worldly
affairs. And carrying out this principle, the
apostle here declares that to do so is a fault.
But when, notwithstanding, he grants his permission to have such cases between brethren
decided in the Church, other brethren adjudi-
cating, and only sternly forbids them to be
carried outside the Church, it is manifest that
here again an indulgence is extended to the
infirmities of the weak. It is in view, then, of
these sins, and others of the same sort, and of
others again more trifling still, which consist of

[164] 1 Cor. vi. 7
[165] Matt. v. 40
[166] Luke vi. 30

offenses in words and thought (as the Apostle James confesses, "In many things we offend all" [167]) that we need to pray every day and often to the Lord, saying, "Forgive us our debts," and to add in truth and sincerity, "as we forgive our debtors."

LXXIX. Sins Which Appear Very Trifling, Are Sometimes in Reality Very Serious

Again, there are some sins which would be considered very trifling, if the Scriptures did not show that they are really very serious. For who would suppose that the man who says to his brother, "Thou fool," is in danger of hell-fire, did not He who is the Truth say so? To the wound, however, He immediately applies the cure, giving a rule for reconciliation with one's offended brother: "Therefore, if thou bring thy gift to the altar, and there rememberest that thy brother hath ought against thee," etc.[168] Again, who would suppose that it was so great a sin to observe days, and months, and times, and years, as those do who are anxious or unwilling to begin anything on certain days, or in certain months or years, because the vain doctrines of men lead them to think such times lucky or unlucky, had we not the means of estimating the greatness of the evil from the

[167] Jas. iii. 2
[168] Matt. v. 22, 23

fear expressed by the apostle, who says to such men, "I am afraid of you, lest I have bestowed upon you labor in vain"? [169]

LXXX. Sins, However Great and Detestable, Seem Trivial When We Are Accustomed to Them

Add to this, that sins, however great and detestable they may be, are looked upon as trivial, or as not sins at all, when men get accustomed to them; and so far does this go, that such sins are not only not concealed, but are boasted of, and published far and wide; and thus, as it is written, "The wicked boasteth of his heart's desire, and blesseth the covetous, whom the Lord abhorreth." [170] Iniquity of this kind is in Scripture called a *cry.* You have an instance in the prophet Isaiah, in the case of the evil vineyard: "He looked for judgment, but behold oppression; for righteousness, but behold a cry." [171] Whence also the expression in *Genesis:* "The cry of Sodom and Gomorrah is great," [172] because in these cities crimes were not only not punished, but were openly committed, as if under the protection of the law. And so in our own times: many forms of sin, though not just the same as those of Sodom and Gomorrah, are now so openly and habitually practised, that

[169] Gal. iv. 10, 11
[170] Ps. x. 3
[171] Isa. v. 7
[172] Gen. xviii. 20

not only dare we not excommunicate a layman, we dare not even degrade a clergyman, for the commission of them. So that when, a few years ago, I was expounding the *Epistle to the Galatians,* in commenting on that very place where the apostle says, "I am afraid of you, lest I have bestowed labor upon you in vain," I was compelled to exclaim, "Woe to the sins of men! for it is only when we are not accustomed to them that we shrink from them: when once we are accustomed to them, though the blood of the Son of God was poured out to wash them away, though they are so great that the kingdom of God is wholly shut against them, constant familiarity leads to the toleration of them all, and habitual toleration leads to the practice of many of them. And grant, O Lord, that we may not come to practise all that we have not the power to hinder." But I shall see whether the extravagance of grief did not betray me into rashness of speech.

LXXXI. There Are Two Causes of Sin, Ignorance and Weakness; and We Need Divine Help to Overcome Both

I shall now say this, which I have often said before in other places of my works. There are two causes that lead to sin: either we do not yet know our duty, or we do not perform the duty that we know. The former is the sin of ignorance, the latter of weakness. Now against

these it is our duty to struggle; but we shall
certainly be beaten in the fight, unless we are
helped by God, not only to see our duty, but
also, when we clearly see it, to make the love
of righteousness stronger in us than the love
of earthly things, the eager longing after which,
or the fear of losing which, leads us with our
eyes open into known sin. In the latter case we
are not only sinners, for we are so even when
we err through ignorance, but we are also trans-
gressors of the law; for we leave undone what
we know we ought to do, and we do what we
know we ought not to do. Wherefore not only
ought we to pray for pardon when we have
sinned, saying, "Forgive us our debts, as we
forgive our debtors;" but we ought to pray
for guidance, that we may be kept from sinning,
saying, "and lead us not into temptation." And
we are to pray to Him of whom the Psalmist
says, "The Lord is my light and my salvation:" [173] my light, for He removes my ignorance;
my salvation, for He takes away my infirmity.

LXXXII. The Mercy of God Is Necessary
to True Repentance

Now even penance itself, when by the law
of the Church there is sufficient reason for its
being gone through, is frequently evaded
through infirmity; for shame is the fear of losing
pleasure when the good opinion of men gives
more pleasure than the righteousness which

[173] Ps. xxvii. 1

leads a man to humble himself in penitence. Wherefore the mercy of God is necessary not only when a man repents, but even to lead him to repent. How else explain what the apostle says of certain persons: "if God peradventure will give them repentance"? [174] And before Peter wept bitterly, we are told by the evangelist, "The Lord turned, and looked upon him." [175]

LXXXIII. The Man Who Despises the Mercy of God Is Guilty of the Sin Against the Holy Spirit

Now the man who, not believing that sins are remitted in the Church, despises this great gift of God's mercy, and persists to the last day of his life in his obstinacy of heart, is guilty of the unpardonable sin against the Holy Spirit, in whom Christ forgives sins.[176] But this difficult question I have discussed as clearly as I could in a book devoted exclusively to this one point.

LXXXIV. The Resurrection of the Body Gives Rise to Numerous Questions

Now, as to the resurrection of the body—not a resurrection such as some have had, who came back to life for a time and died again, but a resurrection to eternal life, as the body of Christ Himself rose again—I do not see how I can dis-

[174] 2 Tim. ii. 25
[175] Luke xxii. 61
[176] Matt. xii. 32

cuss the matter briefly, and at the same time give a satisfactory answer to all the questions that are ordinarily raised about it. Yet that the bodies of all men—both those who have been born and those who shall be born, both those who have died and those who shall die—shall be raised again, no Christian ought to have the shadow of a doubt.

LXXXV. The Case of Abortive Conceptions

Hence in the first place arises a question about abortive conceptions, which have indeed been born in the mother's womb, but not so born that they could be born again. For if we shall decide that these are to rise again, we cannot object to any conclusion that may be drawn in regard to those which are fully formed. Now who is there that is not rather disposed to think that unformed abortions perish, like seeds that have never fructified? But who will dare to deny, though he may not dare to affirm, that at the resurrection every defect in the form shall be supplied, and that thus the perfection which time would have brought shall not be wanting, any more than the blemishes which time did bring shall be present: so that the nature shall neither want anything suitable and in harmony with it that length of days would have added, nor be debased by the presence of anything of an opposite kind that length of days has added; but that what is not yet complete shall be completed, just as what has been injured shall be renewed.

LXXXVI. If They Have Ever Lived, They Must of Course Have Died, and Therefore Shall Have a Share in the Resurrection of the Dead

And therefore the following question may be very carefully inquired into and discussed by learned men, though I do not know whether it is in man's power to resolve it: At what time the infant begins to live in the womb: whether life exists in a latent form before it manifests itself in the motions of the living being. To deny that the young who are cut out limb by limb from the womb, lest if they were left there dead the mother should die too, have never been alive, seems too audacious. Now, from the time that a man begins to live, from that time it is possible for him to die. And if he die, wheresoever death may overtake him, I cannot discover on what principle he can be denied an interest in the resurrection of the dead.

LXXXVII. The Case of Monstrous Births

We are not justified in affirming even of monstrosities, which are born and live, however quickly they may die, that they shall not rise again, nor that they shall rise again in their deformity, and not rather with an amended and perfected body. God forbid that the double-limbed man who was lately born in the East, of whom an account was brought by most trustworthy brethren who had seen him—an account which the presbyter Jerome, of blessed memory, left in writing[177]—God forbid, I say, that we should think that at the resurrection there shall be one man with double limbs, and not two distinct men, as would have been the case had twins been born. And so other births, which, because they have either a superfluity or a defect, or because they are very much deformed, are called *monstrosities*, shall at the resurrection be restored to the normal shape of man; and so each single soul shall possess its own body; and no bodies shall cohere together even though they were born in cohesion, but each separately shall possess all the members which constitute a complete human body.

LXXXVIII. The Material of the Body Never Perishes

Nor does the earthly material out of which men's mortal bodies are created ever perish; but though it may crumble into dust and ashes, or be dissolved into vapors and exhalations, though it may be transformed into the substance of other bodies, or dispersed into the

[177] Jerome, in his *Epistle to Vitalis:* "Or because in our times a man was born at Lydda with two heads, four hands, one belly, and two feet, does it necessearily follow that all men are so born?"

elements, though it should become food for
beasts or men, and be changed into their flesh,
it returns in a moment of time to that human
soul which animated it at the first, and which
caused it to become man, and to live and
grow.

LXXXIX. But This Material May Be Differently Arranged in the Resurrection Body

And this earthly material, which when the
soul leaves it becomes a corpse, shall not at the
resurrection be so restored as that the parts into
which it is separated, and which under various
forms and appearances become parts of other
things (though they shall all return to the same
body from which they were separated) must
necessarily return to the same parts of the body
in which they were originally situated. For
otherwise, to suppose that the hair recovers all
that our frequent clippings and shavings have
taken away from it, and the nails all that we
have so often pared off, presents to the imagination such a picture of ugliness and deformity, as
to make the resurrection of the body all but
incredible. But just as if a statue of some soluble
metal were either melted by fire, or broken into
dust, or reduced to a shapeless mass, and a
sculptor wished to restore it from the same
quantity of metal, it would make no difference
to the completeness of the work what part of
the statue any given particle of the material was

put into, as long as the restored statue contained all the material of the original one; so God, the Artificer of marvellous and unspeakable power, shall with marvellous and unspeakable rapidity restore our body, using up the whole material of which it originally consisted. Nor will it affect the completeness of its restoration whether hairs return to hairs, and nails to nails, or whether the part of these that had perished be changed into flesh, and called to take its place in another part of the body, the great Artist taking careful heed that nothing shall be unbecoming or out of place.

XC. If There Be Differences and Inequalities Among the Bodies of Those Who Rise Again, There Shall Be Nothing Offensive or Disproportionate in Any

Nor does it necessarily follow that there shall be differences of stature among those who rise again, because they were of different statures during life; nor is it certain that the lean shall rise again in their former leanness, and the fat in their former fatness. But if it is part of the Creator's design that each should preserve his own peculiarities of feature, and retain a recognizable likeness to his former self, while in regard to other bodily advantages all should be equal, then the material of which each is composed may be so modified that none of it shall be lost, and that any defect may be supplied by Him who can create at His will out of nothing. But if in the bodies of those who rise again there shall be a well-ordered inequality, such as there is in the voices that make up a full harmony, then the material of each man's body shall be so dealt with that it shall form a man fit for the assemblies of the angels, and one who shall bring nothing among them to jar upon their sensibilities. And assuredly nothing that is unseemly shall be there; but whatever shall be there shall be graceful and becoming: for if anything is not seemly, neither shall it be.

XCI. The Bodies of the Saints Shall at the Resurrection Be Spiritual Bodies

The bodies of the saints, then, shall rise again free from every defect, from every blemish, as from all corruption, weight, and impediment. For their ease of movement shall be as complete as their happiness. Whence their bodies have been called *spiritual*, though undoubtedly they shall be bodies and not spirits. For just as now the body is called *animate*, though it is a body, and not a soul [*anima*], so then the body shall be called spiritual, though it shall be a body, not a spirit.[178] Hence, as far as regards the corruption which now weighs down the soul, and the vices which urge the flesh to lust against the spirit,[179] it shall not then be flesh, but body; for

[178] 1 Cor. xv. 44
[179] Wisd. ix. 15; Gal. v. 17

there are bodies which are called celestial.
Wherefore it is said, "Flesh and blood cannot
inherit the kingdom of God;" and, as if in explanation of this, "neither doth corruption inherit incorruption." [180] What the apostle first
called "flesh and blood," he afterwards calls
"corruption;" and what he first called "the kingdom of God," he afterwards calls "incorruption." But as far as regards the substance, even
then it shall be flesh. For even after the resurrection the body of Christ was called flesh.[181] The
apostle, however, says: "It is sown a natural
body; it is raised a spiritual body;" [182] because
so perfect shall then be the harmony between
flesh and spirit, the spirit keeping alive the
subjugated flesh without the need of any nourishment, that no part of our nature shall be in
discord with another; but as we shall be free
from enemies without, so we shall not have ourselves for enemies within.

XCII. THE RESURRECTION OF THE LOST

But as for those who, out of the mass of
perdition caused by the first man's sin, are not
redeemed through the one Mediator between
God and man, they too shall rise again, each
with his own body, but only to be punished with
the devil and his angels. Now, whether they
shall rise again with all their diseases and de-
formities of body, bringing with them the dis-

[180] 1 Cor. xv. 50
[181] Luke xxiv. 39
[182] 1 Cor. xv. 44

eased and deformed limbs which they possessed here, it would be labor lost to inquire.
For we need not weary ourselves speculating
about their health or their beauty, which are
matters uncertain, when their eternal damnation
is a matter of certainty. Nor need we inquire in
what sense their body shall be incorruptible, if
it be susceptible of pain; or in what sense corruptible, if it be free from the possibility of
death. For there is no true life except where
there is happiness in life, and no true incorruption except where health is unbroken by any
pain. When, however, the unhappy are not
permitted to die, then, if I may so speak, death
itself dies not; and where pain without intermission afflicts the soul, and never comes to an
end, corruption itself is not completed. This is
called in Holy Scripture "the second death." [183]

XCIII. Both the First and the Second Deaths Are the Consequence of Sin. Punishment Is Proportioned to Guilt

And neither the first death, which takes place
when the soul is compelled to leave the body,
nor the second death, which takes place when
the soul is not permitted to leave the suffering
body, would have been inflicted on man had no
one sinned. And, of course, the mildest punishment of all will fall upon those who have added
no actual sin, to the original sin they brought

[183] Rev. ii. 2

with them; and as for the rest who have added
such actual sins, the punishment of each will
be the more tolerable in the next world, according as his iniquity has been less in this world.

XCIV. The Saints Shall Know More Fully in the Next World the Benefits They Have Received by Grace

Thus, when reprobate angels and men are
left to endure everlasting punishment, the saints
shall know more fully the benefits they have
received by grace. Then, in contemplation of
the actual facts, they shall see more clearly the
meaning of the expression in the psalms, "I will
sing of mercy and judgment;" [184] for it is only
of unmerited mercy that any is redeemed, and
only in well-merited judgment that any is condemned.

XCV. God's Judgments Shall Then Be Explained

Then shall be made clear much that is now
dark. For example, when of two infants, whose
cases seem in all respects alike, one is by the
mercy of God chosen to Himself, and the other
is by His justice abandoned (wherein the one
who is chosen may recognize what was of justice
due to himself, had not mercy intervened); why,

[184] Ps. ci. 1

of these two, the one should have been chosen
rather than the other, is to us an insoluble problem. And again, why miracles were not wrought
in the presence of men who would have repented at the working of the miracles, while
they were wrought in the presence of others
who, it was known, would not repent. For our
Lord says most distinctly: "Woe unto thee,
Chorazin! woe unto thee, Bethsaida! for if the
mighty works, which were done in you, had
been done in Tyre and Sidon, they would have
repented long ago in sackcloth and ashes." [185]
And assuredly there was no injustice in God's
not willing that they should be saved, though
they could have been saved had He so willed
it. Then shall be seen in the clearest light of
wisdom what with the pious is now a faith,
though it is not yet a matter of certain knowledge, how sure, how unchangeable, and how
effectual is the will of God; how many things
He can do which He does not will to do, though
willing nothing which He cannot perform; and
how true is the song of the psalmist, "But our
God is in the heavens; He hath done whatsoever
He hath pleased." [186] And this certainly is not
true, if God has ever willed anything that He
has not performed; and, still worse, if it was the
will of man that hindered the Omnipotent from
doing what He pleased. Nothing, therefore,
happens but by the will of the Omnipotent, He
either permitting it to be done, or Himself doing
it.

[185] Matt. xi. 21
[186] Ps. cxv. 3

XCVI. The Omnipotent God Does Well Even in the Permission of Evil

Nor can we doubt that God does well even in the permission of what is evil. For He permits it only in the justice of His judgment. And surely all that is just is good. Although, therefore, evil, in so far as it is evil, is not a good; yet the fact that evil as well as good exists, is a good. For if it were not a good that evil should exist, its existence would not be permitted by the omnipotent God, who without doubt can as easily refuse to permit what He does not wish, as bring about what He does wish. And if we do not believe this, the very first sentence of our creed is endangered, wherein we profess to believe in God the Father Almighty. For He is not truly called Almighty if He cannot do whatsoever He pleases, or if the power of His almighty will is hindered by the will of any creature whatsoever.

XCVII. In What Sense Does the Apostle Say That "God Will Have All Men to Be Saved," When, as a Matter of Fact, All Are Not Saved?

Hence we must inquire in what sense is said of God what the apostle has most truly said: "Who will have all men to be saved." [187] For,

[187] 1 Tim. ii. 4.

as a matter of fact, not all, nor even a majority, are saved: so that it would seem that what God wills is not done, man's will interfering with, and hindering the will of God. When we ask the reason why all men are not saved, the ordinary answer is: "Because men themselves are not willing." This, indeed, cannot be said of infants, for it is not in their power either to will or not to will. But if we could attribute to their will the childish movements they make at baptism, when they make all the resistance they can, we should say that even they are not willing to be saved. Our Lord says plainly, however, in the Gospel, when upbraiding the impious city: "How often would I have gathered thy children together, even as a hen gathereth her chickens under her wings, and ye would not!" [188] as if the will of God had been overcome by the will of men, and when the weakest stood in the way with their want of will, the will of the strongest could not be carried out. And where is that omnipotence which hath done all that it pleased on earth and in heaven, if God willed to gather together the children of Jerusalem, and did not accomplish it? Or rather, Jerusalem was not willing that her children should be gathered together, but even though she was unwilling, He gathered together as many of her children as He wished: for He does not will some things and do them, and will others and do them not; but "He hath done all that He pleased in heaven and in earth."

[188] Matt. xxiii. 37

XCVIII. Predestination to Eternal Life Is Wholly of God's Free Grace

And, moreover, who will be so foolish and blasphemous as to say that God cannot change the evil wills of men, whichever, whenever, and wheresoever He chooses, and direct them to what is good? But when He does this, He does it of mercy; when He does it not, it is of justice that He does it not; for "He hath mercy on whom He will have mercy, and whom He will He hardeneth." [189] And when the apostle said this, he was illustrating the grace of God, in connection with which he had just spoken of the twins in the womb of Rebecca, "who being not yet born, neither having done any good or evil, that the purpose of God according to election might stand, not of works, but of Him that calleth, it was said unto her, The elder shall serve the younger." [190] And in reference to this matter he quotes another prophetic testimony: "Jacob have I loved, but Esau have I hated." [191] But perceiving how what he had said might affect those who could not penetrate by their understanding the depth of this grace: "What shall we say then?" he says: "Is there unrighteousness with God? God forbid." [192] For it seems unjust that, in the absence of any merit or demerit, from good or evil works, God should

[189] Rom. ix. 18
[190] Rom. ix. 12
[191] Rom. ix. 13; Mal. i. 2, 3
[192] Rom. ix. 14

love the one and hate the other. Now, if the apostle had wished us to understand that there were future good works of the one, and evil works of the other, which of course God foreknew, he would never have said, "not of works," but, "of future works," and in that way would have solved the difficulty, or rather there would then have been no difficulty to solve. As it is, however, after answering, "God forbid;" that is, God forbid that there should be unrighteousness with God; he goes on to prove that there is no unrighteousness in God's doing this, and says: "For He saith to Moses, I will have mercy on whom I will have mercy, and I will have compassion on whom I will have compassion." [193] Now, who but a fool would think that God was unrighteous, either in inflicting penal justice on those who had earned it, or in extending mercy to the unworthy? Then he draws his conclusion: "So then it is not of him that willeth, nor of him that runneth, but of God that showeth mercy." [194] Thus both the twins were born children of wrath, not on account of any works of their own, but because they were bound in the fetters of that original condemnation which came through Adam. But He who said, "I will have mercy on whom I will have mercy," loved Jacob of His undeserved grace, and hated Esau of His deserved judgment. And as this judgment was due to both, the former learnt from the case of the latter that the fact of the same punishment not falling

[193] Rom. ix. 15; Ex. xxxiii. 19
[194] Rom. ix. 16

upon himself gave him no room to glory in any merit of his own, but only in the riches of the divine grace; because "it is not of him that willeth, nor of him that runneth, but of God that showeth mercy." And indeed the whole face, and, if I may use the expression, every lineament of the countenance of Scripture conveys by a very profound analogy this wholesome warning to every one who looks carefully into it, that he who glories should glory in the Lord.[195]

XCIX. As God's Mercy Is Free, So His Judgments Are Just, and Cannot Be Gainsaid

Now after commending the mercy of God, saying, "So it is not of him that willeth, nor of him that runneth, but of God that showeth mercy," that he might commend His justice also (for the man who does not obtain mercy finds, not iniquity, but justice, there being no iniquity with God) he immediately adds: "For the scripture saith unto Pharaoh, Even for this same purpose have I raised thee up, that I might show my power in thee, and that my name might be declared throughout all the earth." [196] And then he draws a conclusion that applies to both, that is, both to His mercy and His justice: "Therefore hath He mercy on whom He will have mercy, and whom He will He hardeneth." [197] "He hath mercy" of His great goodness,

[195] cf. 1 Cor. i. 31
[196] Rom. ix. 17; Ex. ix. 16
[197] Rom. ix. 18

"He hardeneth" without any injustice; so that neither can he that is pardoned glory in any merit of his own, nor he that is condemned complain of anything but his own demerit. For it is grace alone that separates the redeemed from the lost, all having been involved in one common perdition through their common origin. Now if any one, on hearing this, should say, "Why doth He yet find fault? for who hath resisted His will?" [198] as if a man ought not to be blamed for being bad, because God hath mercy on whom He will have mercy, and whom He will He hardeneth, God forbid that we should be ashamed to answer as we see the apostle answered: "Nay, but, O man, who art thou that repliest against God? Shall the thing formed say to Him that formed it, Why hast Thou made me thus? Hath not the potter power over the clay, of the same lump to make one vessel unto honor, and another unto dishonor?" [199] Now some foolish people think that in this place the apostle had no answer to give; and for want of a reason to render, rebuked the presumption of his interrogator. But there is great weight in this saying: "Nay, but, O man, who art thou?" and in such a matter as this it suggests to a man in a single word the limits of his capacity, and at the same time does in reality convey an important reason. For if a man does not understand these matters, who is he that he should reply against God? And if he does understand them, he finds no further room

[198] Rom. ix. 19
[199] Rom. ix. 20, 21

for reply. For then he perceives that the whole
human race was condemned in its rebellious
head by a divine judgment so just, that if not a
single member of the race had been redeemed,
no one could justly have questioned the justice
of God; and that it was right that those who
are redeemed should be redeemed in such a
way as to show, by the greater number who are
unredeemed and left in their just condemnation, what the whole race deserved, and whither
the deserved judgment of God would lead even
the redeemed, did not His undeserved mercy
interpose, so that every mouth might be stopped
of those who wish to glory in their own merits,
and that he that glorieth might glory in the
Lord.[200]

C. The Will of God Is Never Defeated, Though Much Is Done That Is Contrary to His Will

These are the great works of the Lord, sought
out according to all His pleasure,[201] and so
wisely sought out, that when the intelligent
creation, both angelic and human, sinned, doing
not His will but their own, He used the very
will of the creature which was working in opposition to the Creator's will as an instrument
for carrying out His will, the supremely Good
thus turning to good account even what is evil,
to the condemnation of those whom in His

[200] Rom. iii. 19; 1 Cor. i. 31
[201] Ps. cxi. 2 (LXX.)

justice He has predestined to punishment, and to the salvation of those whom in His mercy He has predestined to grace. For, as far as relates to their own consciousness, these creatures did what God wished not to be done: but in view of God's omnipotence, they could in no wise effect their purpose. For in the very fact that they acted in opposition to His will, His will concerning them was fulfilled. And hence it is that "the works of the Lord are great, sought out according to all His pleasure," because in a way unspeakably strange and wonderful, even what is done in opposition to His will does not defeat His will. For it would not be done did He not permit it (and of course His permission is not unwilling, but willing); nor would a Good Being permit evil to be done only that in His omnipotence He can turn evil into good.

CI. The Will of God, Which Is Always Good, Is Sometimes Fulfilled Through the Evil Will of Man

Sometimes, however, a man in the goodness of his will desires something that God does not desire, even though God's will is also good, nay, much more fully and more surely good (for His will never can be evil): for example, if a good son is anxious that his father should live, when it is God's good will that he should die. Again, it is possible for a man with evil will to desire what God wills in His goodness: for example, if a bad son wishes his father to die,

when this is also the will of God. It is plain that
the former wishes what God does not wish, and
that the latter wishes what God does wish; and
yet the filial love of the former is more in harmony with the good will of God, though its
desire is different from God's, than the want
of filial affection of the latter, though its desire
is the same as God's. So necessary is it, in de-
termining whether a man's desire is one to be
approved or disapproved, to consider what it
is proper for man, and what it is proper for
God, to desire, and what is in each case the real
motive of the will. For God accomplishes some
of His purposes, which of course are all good,
through the evil desires of wicked men: for
example, it was through the wicked designs of
the Jews, working out the good purpose of the
Father, that Christ was slain; and this event was
so truly good, that when the Apostle Peter expressed his unwillingness that it should take
place, he was designated Satan by Him who had
come to be slain.[202] How good seemed the in-
tentions of the pious believers who were unwilling that Paul should go up to Jerusalem lest
the evils which Agabus had foretold should
there befall him! [203] And yet it was God's purpose that he should suffer these evils for preach-
ing the faith of Christ, and thereby become a
witness for Christ. And this purpose of His,
which was good, God did not fulfill through the
good counsels of the Christians, but through the
evil counsels of the Jews; so that those who

[202] Matt. xvi. 21-23
[203] Acts xxi. 10-12

opposed His purpose were more truly His servants than those who were the willing instru-
ments of its accomplishment; both worked to the
same end, He with His good will through them,
they with their evil will.

CII. The Will of the Omnipotent God Is Never Defeated, and Is Never Evil

But however strong may be the purposes
either of angels or of men, whether of good or
bad, whether these purposes fall in with the will
of God or run counter to it, the will of the
Omnipotent is never defeated; and His will
never can be evil; because even when it inflicts
evil it is just, and what is just is certainly not
evil. The omnipotent God, then, whether in
mercy He pitieth whom He will, or in judgment hardeneth whom He will, is never unjust
in what He does, never does anything except
of His own free-will, and never wills anything
that He does not perform.

CIII. Interpretation of the Expression in I Tim. ii. 4: "Who Will Have All Men to Be Saved"

Accordingly, when we hear and read in Scripture that He "will have all men to be saved," [204]
although we know well that all men are not
saved, we are not on that account to restrict

[204] 1 Tim. ii. 4

the omnipotence of God, but are rather to
understand the Scripture, "Who will have all
men to be saved," as meaning that no man is
saved unless God wills his salvation: not that
there is no man whose salvation He does not
will, but that no man is saved apart from His
will; and that, therefore, we should pray Him
to will our salvation, because if He will it, it
must necessarily be accomplished. And it was
of prayer to God that the apostle was speaking
when he used this expression. And on the same
principle we interpret the expression in the
Gospel: "The true light which lighteth every
man that cometh into the world:" [205] not that
there is no man who is not enlightened, but that
no man is enlightened except by Him. Or, it is
said, "Who will have all men to be saved;" not
that there is no man whose salvation He does
not will (for how, then, explain the fact that
He was unwilling to work miracles in the presence of some who, He said, would have repented
if He had worked them?), but that we are to
understand by "all men," the human race in all
its varieties of rank and circumstances—kings,
subjects; noble, plebeian, high, low, learned,
and unlearned; the sound in body, the feeble,
the clever, the dull, the foolish, the rich, the
poor, and those of middling circumstances;
males, females, infants, boys, youths; young,
middle-aged, and old men; of every tongue, of
every fashion, of all arts, of all professions, with
all the innumerable differences of will and conscience, and whatever else there is that makes

[205] John i. 9

a distinction among men. For which of all these classes is there out of which God does not will that men should be saved in all nations through His only-begotten Son, our Lord, and therefore does save them; for the Omnipotent cannot will in vain, whatsoever He may will? Now the apostle had enjoined that prayers should be made for all men, and had especially added, "For kings, and for all that are in authority," who might be supposed, in the pride and pomp of worldly station, to shrink from the humility of the Christian faith. Then saying, "For this is good and acceptable in the sight of God our Saviour," that is, that prayers should be made for such as these, he immediately adds, as if to remove any ground of despair, "Who will have all men to be saved, and to come unto the knowledge of the truth." [206] God, then, in His great condescension has judged it good to grant to the prayers of the humble the salvation of the exalted; and assuredly we have many examples of this. Our Lord, too, makes use of the same mode of speech in the Gospel, when He says to the Pharisees: "Ye tithe mint, and rue, and every herb." [207] For the Pharisees did not tithe what belonged to others, nor all the herbs of all the inhabitants of other lands. As, then, in this place we must understand by "every herb," every kind of herb, so in the former passage we may understand by "all men," every sort of men. And we may interpret it in any other way we please, so long as we are not com-

[206] 1 Tim. ii. 1-4
[207] Luke xi. 42

pelled to believe that the omnipotent God has
willed anything to be done which was not done:
for, setting aside all ambiguities, if "He hath
done all that He pleased in heaven and in
earth," [208] as the psalmist sings of Him, He
certainly did not will to do anything that He
hath not done.

CIV. God, Foreknowing the Sin of the First Man, Ordered His Own Purposes Accordingly

Wherefore, God would have been willing to
preserve even the first man in that state of
salvation in which he was created, and after
he had begotten sons to remove him at a fit
time, without the intervention of death, to a
better place, where he should have been not
only free from sin, but free even from the desire
of sinning, if He had foreseen that man would
have the steadfast will to persist in the state of
innocence in which he was created. But as He
foresaw that man would make a bad use of his
free-will, that is, would sin, God arranged His
own designs rather with a view to do good
to man even in his sinfulness, that thus the
good will of the Omnipotent might not be made
void by the evil will of man, but might be fulfilled in spite of it.

[208] Ps. cxv. 3

CV. Man Was So Created as to Be Able to Choose Either Good or Evil: in the Future Life, the Choice of Evil Will Be Impossible

Now it was expedient that man should be at first so created, as to have it in his power both to will what was right and to will what was wrong; not without reward if he willed the former, and not without punishment if he willed the latter. But in the future life it shall not be in his power to will evil; and yet this will constitute no restriction on the freedom of his will. On the contrary, his will shall be much freer when it shall be wholly impossible for him to be the slave of sin. We should never think of blaming the will, or saying that it was no will, or that it was not to be called free, when we so desire happiness, that not only do we shrink from misery, but find it utterly impossible to do otherwise. As, then, the soul even now finds it impossible to desire unhappiness, so in the future it shall be wholly impossible for it to desire sin. But God's arrangement was not to be broken, according to which He willed to show how good is a rational being who is able even to refrain from sin, and yet how much better is one who cannot sin at all; just as that was an inferior sort of immortality, and yet it was immortality, when it was possible for man to avoid death, although there is reserved for the future a more perfect immortality, when it shall be impossible for man to die.

CVI. The Grace of God Was Necessary to Man's Salvation Before the Fall as Well as After It

The former immortality man lost through the exercise of his free-will; the latter he shall obtain through grace, whereas, if he had not sinned, he should have obtained it by desert. Even in that case, however, there could have been no merit without grace; because, although the mere exercise of man's free-will was sufficient to bring in sin, his free-will would not have sufficed for his maintenance in righteousness, unless God had assisted it by imparting a portion of His unchangeable goodness. Just as it is in man's power to die whenever he will (for, not to speak of other means, any one can put an end to himself by simple abstinence from food), but the mere will cannot preserve life in the absence of food and the other means of life; so man in paradise was able of his mere will, simply by abandoning righteousness, to destroy himself; but to have maintained a life of right-eousness would have been too much for his will, unless it had been sustained by the Creator's power. After the fall, however, a more abundant exercise of God's mercy was required, because the will itself had to be freed from the bondage in which it was held by sin and death. And the will owes its freedom in no degree to itself, but solely to the grace of God which comes by faith in Jesus Christ; so that the very will, through

which we accept all the other gifts of God
which lead us on to His eternal gift, is itself
prepared of the Lord, as the Scripture says.[209]

CVII. Eternal Life, Though the Reward of Good Works, Is Itself the Gift of God

Wherefore, even eternal life itself, which is
surely the reward of good works, the apostle
calls the gift of God. "For the wages of sin," he
says, "is death; but the gift of God is eternal life
through Jesus Christ our Lord." [210] Wages is
paid as a recompense for military service; it
is not a gift: wherefore he says, "the *wages* of
sin is death," to show that death was not inflicted
undeservedly, but as the due recompense of sin.
But a gift, unless it is wholly unearned, is not
a gift at all.[211] We are to understand, then,
that man's good deserts are themselves the gift
of God, so that when these obtain the recompense of eternal life, it is simply grace given
for grace. Man, therefore, was thus made upright
that, though unable to remain in his uprightness
without divine help, he could of his own mere
will depart from it. And whichever of these
courses he had chosen, God's will would have
been done, either by him, or concerning him.
Therefore, as he chose to do his own will rather
than God's, the will of God is fulfilled concerning him; for God, out of one and the same heap
of perdition which constitutes the race of man,

[209] Prov. xvi. 1
[210] Rom. vi. 23
[211] Rom. xi. 6

makes one vessel to honor, another to dishonor;
to honor in mercy, to dishonor in judgment;[212]
that no one may glory in man, and consequently
not in himself.

CVIII. A Mediator Was Necessary to Reconcile Us to God; and Unless This Mediator Had Been God, He Could Not Have Been Our Redeemer

For we could not be redeemed, even through
the one Mediator between God and men, the
man Christ Jesus, if He were not also God.
Now when Adam was created, he, being a
righteous man, had no need of a mediator. But
when sin had placed a wide gulf between God
and the human race, it was expedient that a
Mediator, who alone of the human race was
born, lived, and died without sin, should reconcile us to God, and procure even for our bodies
a resurrection to eternal life, in order that the
pride of man might be exposed and cured
through the humility of God; that man might
be shown how far he had departed from God,
when God became incarnate to bring him back;
that an example might be set to disobedient man
in the life of obedience of the God-Man; that
the fountain of grace might be opened by the
Only-begotten taking upon Himself the form
of a servant, a form which had no antecedent
merit; that an earnest of that resurrection of
the body which is promised to the redeemed

[212] Rom. ix 21

might be given in the resurrection of the Redeemer; that the devil might be subdued by the
same nature which it was his boast to have
deceived, and yet man not glorified, lest pride
should again spring up; and, in fine, with a view
to all the advantages which the thoughtful can
perceive and describe, or perceive without being
able to describe, as flowing from the transcend-
ent mystery of the person of the Mediator.

CIX. The State of the Soul During the Interval Between Death and the Resurrection

During the time, moreover, which intervenes
between a man's death and the final resurrection,
the soul dwells in a hidden retreat, where it
enjoys rest or suffers affliction just in proportion
to the merit it has earned by the life which it
led on earth.

CX. The Benefit to the Souls of the Dead From the Sacraments and Alms of Their Living Friends

Nor can it be denied that the souls of the
dead are benefited by the piety of their living
friends, who offer the sacrifice of the Mediator,
or give alms in the church on their behalf. But
these services are of advantage only to those
who during their lives have earned such merit,
that services of this kind can help them. For

there is a manner of life which is neither so
good as not to require these services after death,
nor so bad that such services are of no avail
after death; there is, on the other hand, a kind
of life so good as not to require them; and again,
one so bad that when life is over they render no
help. Therefore, it is in this life that all the
merit or demerit is acquired, which can either
relieve or aggravate a man's sufferings after
this life. No one, then, need hope that after he
is dead he shall obtain merit with God which
he has neglected to secure here. And accordingly
it is plain that the services which the church
celebrates for the dead are in no way opposed
to the apostle's words: "For we must all appear
before the judgment-seat of Christ; that every
one may receive the things done in his body,
according to that he hath done, whether it be
good or bad;" [213] for the merit which renders
such services as I speak of profitable to a man,
is earned while he lives in the body. It is not
to every one that these services are profitable.
And why are they not profitable to all, except
because of the different kinds of lives that men
lead in the body? When, then, sacrifices either
of the altar or of alms are offered on behalf of
all the baptized dead, they are thank-offerings
for the very good, they are propitiatory offerings for the not very bad, and in the case of the
very bad, even though they do not assist the
dead, they are a species of consolation to the
living. And where they are profitable, their
benefit consists either in obtaining a full remis-

[213] 2 Cor. v. 10; cf. Rom. xiv. 10

sion of sins, or at least in making the condemnation more tolerable.

CXI. AFTER THE RESURRECTION THERE SHALL BE TWO DISTINCT KINGDOMS, ONE OF ETERNAL HAPPINESS, THE OTHER OF ETERNAL MISERY

After the resurrection, however, when the final, universal judgment has been completed, two groups of citizens, one Christ's, the other the devil's, shall have fixed lots; one consisting of the good, the other of the bad—both, however, consisting of angels and men. The former shall have no will, the latter no power, to sin, and neither shall have any power to choose death; but the former shall live truly and happily in eternal life, the latter shall drag a miserable existence in eternal death without the power of dying; for both shall be without end. But among the former there shall be degrees of happiness, one being more pre-eminently happy than another; and among the latter there shall be degrees of misery, one being more endurably miserable than another.

CXII. THERE IS NO GROUND IN SCRIPTURE FOR THE OPINION OF THOSE WHO DENY THE ETERNITY OF FUTURE PUNISHMENTS

It is in vain, then, that some, indeed very many, make moan over the eternal punishment,

and perpetual, unintermitted torments of the
lost, and say they do not believe it shall be so;
not, indeed, that they directly oppose themselves
to Holy Scripture, but, at the suggestion of their
own feelings, they soften down everything that
seems hard, and give a milder turn to statements
which they think are rather designed to terrify
than to be received as literally true. For "God,"
they say, "will not forget to be gracious, nor will
He, in anger, shut up His tender mercies." [214]
Now, they read this in one of the holy psalms.
But without doubt we are to understand it as
spoken of those who are elsewhere called "vessels
of mercy," [215] because even they are freed from
misery not on account of any merit of their own,
but solely through the pity of God. Or, if the
men we speak of insist that this passage applies
to all mankind, there is no reason why they
should therefore suppose that there will be an
end to the punishment of those of whom it is
said, "These shall go away into everlasting punishment;" for this shall end in the same manner
and at the same time as the happiness of those
of whom it is said, "but the righteous unto life
eternal." [216] But let them suppose, if the thought
gives them pleasure, that the pains of the damned
are, at certain intervals, in some degree assuaged.
For even in this case the wrath of God, that is,
their condemnation (for it is this, and not any
disturbed feeling in the mind of God that is
called His wrath) abideth upon them;[217] that

[214] Ps. lxxvii. 9
[215] Rom. ix. 23
[216] Matt. xxv. 46
[217] John iii. 36

is, His wrath, though it still remains, does not shut up His tender mercies; though His tender mercies are exhibited, not in putting an end to their eternal punishment, but in mitigating, or in granting them a respite from, their torments; for the psalm does not say, "to put an end to His anger," or, "when His anger is passed by," but "in His anger." [218] Now, if this anger stood alone, or if it existed in the smallest conceivable degree, yet to be lost out of the kingdom of God, to be an exile from the city of God, to be alienated from the life of God, to have no share in that great goodness which God hath laid up for them that fear Him, and hath wrought out for them that trust in Him,[219] would be a punishment so great, that, supposing it to be eternal, no torments that we know of, continued through as many ages as man's imagination can conceive, could be compared with it.

CXIII. The Death of the Wicked Shall Be Eternal in the Same Sense as the Life of the Saints

This perpetual death of the wicked, then, that is, their alienation from the life of God, shall abide for ever, and shall be common to them all, whatever men, prompted by their human affections, may conjecture as to a variety of punishments, or as to a mitigation or intermission of their woes; just as the eternal life of the saints

[218] Ps. lxxviii.
[219] Ps. xxxi. 19

shall abide for ever, and shall be common to
them all, whatever grades of rank and honor
there may be among those who shine with an
harmonious effulgence.

CXIV. Having Dealt With Faith, We Now Come to Speak of Hope. Everything That Pertains to Hope Is Embraced in the Lord's Prayer

Out of this confession of *faith*, which is briefly
comprehended in the Creed, and which, carnally
understood, is milk for babies, but, spiritually
apprehended and studied, is meat for strong
men, springs the good *hope* of believers; and this
is accompanied by a holy *love*. But of these
matters, all of which are true objects of faith,
those only pertain to hope which are embraced
in the Lord's Prayer. For, "Cursed is the man
that trusteth in man" [220] is the testimony of holy
writ; and, consequently, this curse attaches also
to the man who trusteth in himself. Therefore,
except from God the Lord we ought to ask for
nothing either that we hope to do well, or hope
to obtain as a reward of our good works.

CXV. The Seven Petitions of the Lord's Prayer, According to Matthew

Accordingly, in the Evangelist Matthew the
Lord's Prayer seems to embrace seven petitions,
three of which ask for eternal blessings, and the

[220] Jer. xvii. 5

remaining four for temporal; these latter, however, being necessary antecedents to the attainment of the eternal. For when we say, "Hallowed
be Thy name: Thy Kingdom come: Thy will be
done in earth, as it is in heaven" [221] (which
some have interpreted, not unfairly, in body as
well as in spirit) we ask for blessings that are
to be enjoyed for ever; which are indeed begun
in this world, and grow in us as we grow in
grace, but in their perfect state, which is to be
looked for in another life, shall be a possession
for evermore. But when we say, "Give us this day
our daily bread: and forgive us our debts, as
we forgive our debtors: and lead us not into
temptation, but deliver us from evil," [222] who
does not see that we ask for blessings that have
reference to the wants of this present life? In
that eternal life, where we hope to live for ever,
the hallowing of God's name, and His kingdom,
and His will in our spirit and body, shall be
brought to perfection, and shall endure to everlasting. But our daily bread is so called because
there is here constant need for as much nourishment as the spirit and the flesh demand, whether
we understand the expression spiritually, or carnally, or in both senses. It is here too that we
need the forgiveness that we ask, for it is here
that we commit the sins; here are the temptations
which allure or drive us into sin; here, in a word,
is the evil from which we desire deliverance: but
in that other world there shall be none of these
things.

[221] Matt. vi. 9, 10
[222] Matt. vi. 11-13

CXVI. Luke Expresses the Substance of These Seven Petitions More Briefly in Five

But the Evangelist Luke in his version of the Lord's Prayer embraces not seven, but five petitions: not, of course, that there is any discrepancy between the two evangelists, but that Luke indicates by his very brevity the mode in which the seven petitions of Matthew are to be understood. For God's name is hallowed in the spirit; and God's kingdom shall come in the resurrection of the body. Luke, therefore, intending to show that the third petition is a sort of repetition of the first two, has chosen to indicate that by omitting the third altogether. Then he adds three others: one for daily bread, another for pardon of sin, another for immunity from temptation. And what Matthew puts as the last petition, "but deliver us from evil," Luke has omitted, to show us that it is embraced in the previous petition about temptation. Matthew, indeed, himself says, "*but* deliver," not "*and* deliver," as if to show that the petitions are virtually one: do not this, but this; so that every man is to understand that he is delivered from evil in the very fact of his not being led into temptation.

CXVII. Love, Which Is Greater Than Faith and Hope, Is Shed Abroad in Our Hearts by the Holy Spirit

And now as to *love*, which the apostle declares to be greater than the other two graces, that is, than faith and hope,[223] the greater the measure in which it dwells in a man, the better is tho man in whom it dwells. For when there is a question as to whether a man is good, one does not ask what he believes, or what he hopes, but what he loves. For the man who loves aright no doubt believes and hopes aright; whereas the man who has not love believes in vain, even though his beliefs are true; and hopes in vain, even though the objects of his hope are a real part of true happiness; unless, indeed, he believes and hopes for this, that he may obtain by prayer the blessing of love. For, although it is not possible to hope without love, it may yet happen that a man does not love that which is necessary to the attainment of his hope; as, for example, if he hopes for eternal life (and who is there that does not desire this?) and yet does not love righteousness, without which no one can attain to eternal life. Now this is the true faith of Christ which the apostle speaks of, "which worketh by love;" [224] and if there is anything that it does not yet embrace in its love, asks that it may receive, seeks that it may find, and knocks that

[223] 1 Cor. xiii. 13
[224] Gal. v. 6

it may be opened unto it.[225] For faith obtains through prayer that which the law commands. For without the gift of God, that is, without the Holy Spirit, through whom love is shed abroad in our hearts,[226] the law can command, but it cannot assist; and, moreover, it makes a man a transgressor, for he can no longer excuse himself on the plea of ignorance. Now carnal lust reigns where there is not the love of God.

CXVIII. The Four Stages of the Christian's Life, and the Four Corresponding Stages of the Church's History

When, sunk in the darkest depths of ignorance, man lives according to the flesh, undisturbed by any struggle of reason, this is his first state. Afterwards, when through the law has come the knowledge of sin, and the Spirit of God has not yet interposed His aid, man, striving to live according to the law, is thwarted in his efforts and falls into conscious sin, and so, being overcome of sin, becomes its slave ("for of whom a man is overcome, of the same is he brought in bondage" [227]); and thus the effect produced by the knowledge of the commandment is this, that sin worketh in man all manner of concupiscence, and he is involved in the additional guilt of willful transgression, and that is fulfilled which is written: "The law entered that the offense

[225] Matt. vii. 7
[226] Rom. v. 5
[227] 2 Pet. ii. 19

might abound." [228] This is man's second state. But if God has regard to him, and inspires him with faith in God's help, and the Spirit of God begins to work in him, then the mightier power of love strives against the power of the flesh; and although there is still in the man's own nature a power that fights against him (for his disease is not completely cured), yet he lives the life of the just by faith, and lives in righteousness so far as he does not yield to evil lust, but conquers it by the love of holiness. This is the third state of a man of good hope; and he who by steadfast piety advances in this course, shall attain at last to peace, that peace which, after this life is over, shall be perfected in the repose of the spirit, and finally in the resurrection of the body. Of these four different stages the first is before the law, the second is under the law, the third is under grace, and the fourth is in full and perfect peace. Thus, too, has the history of God's people been ordered according to His pleasure who disposeth all things in number, and measure, and weight. [229] For they existed at first before the law; then under the law, which was given by Moses; then under grace, which was first made manifest in the coming of the Mediator. Not, indeed, that this grace was absent previously, but, in harmony with the arrangements of the time, it was veiled and hidden. For none, even of the just men of old, could find salvation apart from the faith of Christ; nor unless He had been known to them

[228] Rom. v. 20
[229] Wisd. xi. 20

could their ministry have been used to convey prophecies concerning Him to us, some more plain, and some more obscure.

CXIX. The Grace of Regeneration Washes Away All Past Sin and All Original Guilt

Now in whichever of these four stages (as we may call them) the grace of regeneration finds any particular man, all his past sins are there and then pardoned, and the guilt which he contracted in his birth is removed in his new birth; and so true is it that "the wind bloweth where it listeth," [230] that some have never known the second stage, that of slavery under the law, but have received the divine assistance as soon as they received the commandment.

CXX. Death Cannot Injure Those Who Have Received the Grace of Regeneration

But before a man can receive the commandment, it is necessary that he should live according to the flesh. But if once he has received the sacrament of regeneration, death shall not injure him, even if he should forthwith depart from this life; "for to this end Christ both died, and rose, and revived, that He might be Lord both of the dead and the living;" [231] nor shall death retain dominion over him for whom Christ freely died.

[230] John iii. 8
[231] Rom. xiv. 9

CXXI. Love Is the End of All the Commandments, and God Himself Is Love

All the commandments of God, then, are embraced in love, of which the apostle says: "Now the end of the commandment is charity, out of a pure heart, and of a good conscience, and of faith unfeigned." [232] Thus the end of every commandment is charity, that is, every commandment has love for its aim. But whatever is done either through fear of punishment or from some other carnal motive, and has not for its principle that love which the Spirit of God sheds abroad in the heart, is not done as it ought to be done, however it may appear to men. For this love embraces both the love of God and the love of our neighbor, and "on these two commandments hang all the law and the prophets," [233] we may add the Gospel and the apostles. For it is from these that we hear this voice: "The end of the commandment is charity," and "God is love." [234] Wherefore, all God's commandments, one of which is, "Thou shalt not commit adultery," [235] and all those precepts which are not commandments but special counsels, one of which is, "It is good for a man not to touch a woman," [236] are rightly carried out only when the motive principle of action is the love of God, and the

[232] 1 Tim. i. 5
[233] Matt. xxii. 40; Rom. v. 5
[234] 1 Tim. i. 5; 1 John iv. 16
[235] Matt. v. 27 and Rom. xiii. 9
[236] 1 Cor. vii. 1

love of our neighbor in God. And this applies
both to the present and the future life. We love
God now by faith, then we shall love Him
through sight. Now we love even our neighbor
by faith; for we who are ourselves mortal know
not the hearts of mortal men. But in the future
life, the Lord "both will bring to light the hidden
things of darkness, and will make manifest the
counsels of the hearts, and then shall every man
have praise of God;" [237] for every man shall love
and praise in his neighbor the virtue which, that
it may not be hid, the Lord Himself shall bring
to light. Moreover, lust diminishes as love grows,
till the latter grows to such a height that it can
grow no higher here. For "greater love hath no
man than this, that a man lay down his life for
his friends." [238] Who then can tell how great
love shall be in the future world, when there
shall be no lust for it to restrain and conquer?
for that will be the perfection of health when
there shall be no struggle with death.

CXXII. Conclusion

But now there must be an end at last to this
volume. And it is for yourself to judge whether
you should call it a *hand-book,* or should use
it as such. I, however, thinking that your zeal
in Christ ought not to be despised, and believing
and hoping all good of you in dependence on
our Redeemer's help, and loving you very much

[237] 1 Cor. iv. 5
[238] John xv. 13

as one of the members of His body, have, to the best of my ability, written this book for you on *Faith, Hope, and Love*. May its value be equal to its length.

APPENDIX

ANALYSIS AND HISTORICAL APPRAISAL OF THE *ENCHIRIDION*

BY ADOLPH VON HARNACK

IT HAS BEEN attempted to depict Augustine's significance as Church teacher, by dividing absolutely the various directions in which his thought moved, and by giving separate accounts of the Neoplatonist, the Paulist, the earlier Manichaean, and the Catholic Bishop. But it is to be feared that violence is done him by such an analysis. It is safer and more appropriate, within the limits of a history of dogma, to keep to the external unity which he has himself given to his conceptions. In that case his *Enchiridion ad Laurentium*, his matured exposition of the Symbol, presents itself as our best guide. . . . Everything is combined in this book to instruct us as to the nature of the revision (and on the other hand of the confirmation) by Augustine of the popular Catholic dogmatic doctrine that gave a new impress to the Western Church. We shall proceed first to give a minute analysis of the book, and then to set down systematically what was new and at the same time lasting.

Augustine begins by saying that the wisdom of man is piety ("hominis sapientia pietas est" or more accurately "θεοσέβεια") (2). The answer to the question how God is to be worshipped, is—by faith, hope, and love. We have accordingly to determine what is meant by each of these three virtues (3). In them is comprised the whole doctrine of Religion. They cannot, however, be established by reason or perception, but must be derived from Holy Scripture, and be implicitly *believed in* on the testimony of the sacred writers (4). When the soul has attained this faith, it will, if faith works in love, strive to reach that *vision* by which holy and perfected souls perceive the ineffable beauty, the complete contemplation of which is supreme blessedness. "The beginning in faith, the completion in sight, the foundation Christ." But Christ is the foundation only of the Catholic faith, although heretics also call themselves by his name. The evidence for this exclusive relationship between Christ and the Catholic Church would carry us too far here (5). We do not intend to enter into controversy, but to expound (6). The *Symbol* and the *Lord's Prayer* constitute the contents of faith (symbol), and of hope and love (prayer); but faith also prays (7). Faith applies also to things which we do not hope for, but fear; and further to our own affairs and those of others. So far as it—like hope—refers to invisible, future blessings, it is itself hope. But without love it profits nothing, because the devils also believe. Thus everything is comprehended in *faith, which works by love and possesses hope* (8).

Augustine now passes to the Symbol (the ancient Apostolic creed), in order to state the contents of faith. In §§ 9-32, he deals with the first article. The knowledge of nature and physics does *not* belong to faith—besides, scholars con-

jecture rather than know in this matter (opinantes
quam scientes). It is enough for the Christian to
believe that the goodness of the creator is simply
the first cause of all things, so that there is no
nature unless either it is he himself, or is of
him. Further, that this creator is the "Trinity,
supremely and equally, and unchangeably good"
(trinitas summe et æquabiliter et immutabiliter
bona), and that while created things do not
possess this quality, they are good; nay, everything collectively is very good, and produces a
wonderful beauty, in which evil, set in its right
place, only throws the good into relief (9, 10).
Augustine at once passes to the doctrine of evil.
God permits it only because he is so powerful
that he can make good out of evil, *i.e.*, he can
restore the defect of the good (privatio boni),
evil being represented as such defect (morbus
[disease] vulnus [wound]). In the notion of that
which is not supremely good (non summum
bonum esse) we have the capacity for deteriora-
tion; but the good, which is involved in the
existence of any substance, cannot be annihilated,
unless the substance itself be destroyed. But in
that case corruption itself also ceases, since it
can never exist save in what is good: evil can
only exist in what is good (in a *bonum*). This is
expounded at length (11-15). The causes of
good and evil must be known, in order to escape
the errors and infirmities (ærumnæ) of this
life. On the other hand, the causes of great
movements in nature—Augustine returns to § 9—
need not be known; we do not even know the

conditions of our health, which yet lie nearest us (16)!

But is not every error an evil, and what are we to think of deception, lying? These questions are minutely discussed in §§ 17-22. Every case of ignorance is not an error, but only supposed knowledge is, and every error is not hurtful; there is even a good error, one that is of use. But since it is unseemly (deforme atque indecens) for the mind to hold the truth to be false, and the uncertain certain, our life is for that very reason wretched, because at times we need error that we may not lose our life. Such will not be that existence, "where truth itself will be the life of our soul" (ubi ipsa veritas vita animæ nostræ erit). But the lie is worst, so bad that even liars themselves hate being lied to. But yet falsehood offers a difficult problem. (The question of lying in an emergency, whether it can become a duty for a righteous man, is elaborately discussed.) Here again the most important point is to determine wherein one errs: *"it is far more tolerable to lie in those things that are unconnected with religion than to be deceived in those without belief in, or knowledge of, which God cannot be worshipped"* (18).[1] Looked at accurately, every error is an evil, though often, certainly, a small one. It is possible to doubt whether every error is also sinful—*e.g.*, a con-

---

[1] "Longe tolerabilius est in his quæ a religione sunt sejuncta mentiri, quam in iis, sine quorum fide vel notitia deus coli non potest, falli." *E.g.*, to tell anyone falsely that a dead man is still alive is a much less evil than to believe erroneously that Christ will die once more.

fusion about twins, or holding sweet to be bitter,
etc.; at all events, in such cases the sin is exceed-
ingly small and trivial (minimum et levissimum
peccatum), since it has nothing to do with the
way that leads to God, *i.e.* with the faith that
works in love. Error is, indeed, rather an evil than
a sin, a sign of the misery of this life. In any
case, however, we may not, in order to avoid
all error, seek to hold nothing to be true—like
the Academicians; for it is our duty to *believe*.
Besides the standpoint of absolute nescience is
impracticable; for even he who knows not must
deduce his existence from this consciousness of
nescience (20). We must, on the contrary, avoid
the lie; for even when we err in our thought,
we must always say what we think.[1] Even the
lie which benefits another is sinful, although
men who have lied for the general advantage
have contributed a great deal to prosperity (22).
Augustine returns to § 16: we must know the
causes of good and evil. The sole first cause of
the good is the goodness of God; the cause of
evil is the revolt of the will from the unchangeable God on the part of a being, good but
changeable, first, an angel, then man (23). From
this revolt follow all the other infirmities of the
soul [ignorance, concupiscence, etc.] (24). But
the craving for blessedness (appetitus beati-
tudinis) was not lost.

We now have an exposition of Adam's endow-
ment, the Fall, *original sin,* the sentence of death,

[1] C. 22. "Et utique verba propterea sunt instituta, non
per quæ se homines invicem fallunt, sed per quæ in
alterius quisque notitiam cogitationes suas perferat."
(Compare Talleyrand).

the *massa damnata*, which suffers along with the doomed angels, etc. God's goodness is shown, however, in his grant of continued existence to the wicked angels, for whom there is no conversion besides, and in his preservation of men. Although it would have been only justice to give them also over to eternal punishment, he resolved to bring good out of evil (25-27). It was his merciful intention, *i.e.*, to supplement from mankind the number of the angels who persevered in goodness, rendered incomplete by the fall of some, in order that the heavenly Jerusalem might retain its full complement, nay, should be increased by the "sons of our Holy Mother" [filii sanctæ matris] (28-29). But the men chosen owe this not to the merits of their own works (to free will); for in themselves they are dead like the rest (suicides), and are only free to commit sin. Before they are made free, accordingly, they are slaves; they can only be redeemed by grace and faith. Even faith is God's gift, and works will not fail to follow it. Thus they only become free, when God fashions them anew (into the *nova creatura*), producing the act of will as well as its accomplishment ("quamvis non possit credere, sperare, diligere homo rationalis, nisi velit"—although rational man cannot believe, hope, or love, unless he will).[1] That is, God makes the will itself good (misericordia præveniens) and constantly assists it [miseric. subsequens] (30-32).

The exposition of the second article follows

---

[1] C. 32: "Ex utroque fit, id est, ex voluntate homini* et misericordia dei."

in §§ 33-55. Since all men are by nature children
of wrath, and are burdened by original sin and
their own sins, a mediator (reconciliator) was
necessary, who should appease this wrath (justa
vindicta) by presenting a unique sacrifice. That
this was done, and we from being enemies became children, constitutes the grace of God
through Jesus Christ (33). We know that this
mediator is the "Word" that became flesh. The
Word was not transformed, but assumed our
complete human nature from the virgin, being
conceived not by the *libido matris,* but by faith
—and therefore sinlessly.[1] The mother remained
a virgin in giving birth (in partu) (34). We
have now a short discussion on Christ as "God
and man in unity of person, equal to God, and

---

[1] Augustine's whole conception of the sinfulness mingled
with all procreation, and his view that sexual desire is due
not to nature as originally created, but to sin, have admit-
tedly their roots in the earliest period. But they were expressed with Augustine's thoroughness only by the Gnostics, Marcion and—the author of the fragment *De resurrec-
tione* ascribed to Justin. The parallel offered by the latter
(c. 3) is extremely striking. There is not yet, naturally, any
question of sin being propagated through sexual union;
that union is held simply to be sinful; μήτρας ἐστὶν ἐνέργεια
τὸ κυΐσκειν καὶ μορίου ἀνδρικοῦ τὸ σπερμαίνειν· ὥσπερ δέ, εἰ ταῦτα
μέλλει ἐνεργεῖν ταύτας τὰς ἐνεργείας, οὕτως οὐκ ἀναγκαῖον αὐτοῖς
ἐστιν τὸ τὴν ἀρχὴν ἐνεργεῖν (ὁρῶμεν γοῦν πολλὰς γυναῖκας μὴ
κυΐσκούσας, ὡς τὰς στείρας, καὶ μήτρας ἐχούσας), οὕτως οὐκ
εὐθέως καὶ τὸ μήτραν ἔχειν καὶ κυΐσκειν ἀναγκάζει· ἀλλὰ καὶ μὴ
στεῖραι μὲν ἐξ ἀρχῆς, παρθενεύουσαι δέ, κατήργησαν καὶ τὴν
συνουσίαν, ἕτεραι δὲ καὶ ἀπὸ χρόνου· καὶ τοὺς ἄρσενας δὲ τοὺς μὲν
ἀπ᾽ ἀρχῆς παρθενεύοντας ἄρωμεν, τοὺς δὲ ἀπὸ χρόνου, ὥστε δι᾽
αὐτῶν καταλύεσθαι τὸν δι᾽ ἐπιθυμίας ἄνομον γάμον· There are
also beasts that refrain from having connection, ὥστε καὶ δι
ἀνθρώπων καὶ δι᾽ ἀλόγων καταργουμένην συνουσίαν πρὶν τοῦ
μέλλοντος αἰῶνος ὁρᾶσθαι· καὶ ὁ κύριος δὲ ἡμῶν Ἰησοῦς ὁ Χριστὸς
οὐ δι᾽ ἄλλο τι ἐκ παρθένου ἐγεννήθη, ἀλλ᾽ ἵνα καταργήσῃ γέννησιν
ἐπιθυμίας ἀνόμου καὶ δείξῃ τῷ ἄρχοντι καὶ δίχα συνουσίας ἀνθρω-
πίνης δυνατὴν εἶναι τῷ θεῷ τὴν ἀνθρώπου πλάσιν·

as man less than God" (35). Christ, the man
who was deemed worthy to be assumed by
God to form one person with him, is the most
splendid example of grace given *gratis,* and not
according to merits. The same grace that fell
to the man Christ and made him sinless falls
to us in justification from sins. It also revealed
itself in Christ's miraculous birth, in connection
with which, besides, the Holy Ghost did not act
like a natural father. It was rather the whole
Trinity that created the offspring of the virgin:
the man Jesus, like the world, is the creation
of the Trinity. But why precisely the Holy
Ghost is named, it is hard to say. In any case,
the man Jesus was not the son of the Spirit, but
the latter is probably named in order to point
to the grace that, existing without any pre-
ceding merits, had become in the man Jesus
an attribute which in some way was natural
(quodammodo naturalis); for the Holy Spirit
is "so far God that he may be called the gift of
God" [sic deus, ut dicatur etiam dei donum]
(36-40). This is followed again by a long section (41 to 52) on sin and the relation of
Christ to it. Christ was free from original
and actual sin, but was himself—on account of
similarity to sinful flesh—absolutely called sin.
That is, he became a sacrifice for sin, representing
our sin in the flesh in which he was crucified,
"that in some way he might die to sin, in dying
to the flesh,"[1] and from the Resurrection might

[1] "Ut quodammodo peccato moreretur, dum moritur
carni."

seal our new life (41). That is bestowed on us
in baptism. *Everyone* dies to sin in baptism—
even the children, who die to original sin—and
in this respect sin is to be understood collectively;
for even in Adam's sin many forms of sin were
contained. But children are obviously infected
not only by Adam's sin, but also by those of
their parents. For their birth is corrupt, because
by Adam's sin *nature was perverted;* moreover
the actual sins of parents "although they cannot
thus change nature, impose guilt on the children"
(etsi non ita possunt mutare naturam, reatu
tamen obligant filios). But Augustine refrains
from deciding how far the sins of ancestors
project their influence in the chain of descent.
It is all expiated by the mediator, the man Jesus
Christ, who was alone equipped with such grace
as not to need regeneration; for he only accepted
baptism by John in order to give a grand example
of humility, just as he also submitted to death,
not from compulsion, but in order to let the
devil receive his rights (42-49). Christ is thus
Adam's anti-type; but the latter only introduced
one sin into the world, while Christ took away all
that had since been committed. All were condemned in Adam; none escapes the condemnation without Christ. Baptism is to be solemnized
as "the grand mystery in the cross of Christ"
(mysterium grande in cruce Christi); for according to Paul baptism is "nothing but the
similitude of Christ's death; but the death of
Christ crucified is nothing but the similitude of
the remission of sin, that as in him a true death

took place, so in us a true remission of sins." [1]
This is elaborated in accordance with Rom.
VI; we are dead to sin through baptism (50-
52). The clauses of the Symbol are now enu-
merated down to the "sitting at the right hand"
with the observation: *It was so carried out that
in these matters the Christian life which is borne
here should be typified not only mystically by
words but also by deeds.* [2] That is established
in connection with each separate article. Thus
the "sitting at the right hand" means: "set your
affections on those things that are above" (quæ
sursum sunt sapite). On the other hand, the
Return of Christ has no reference to *our* earthly
life. It belongs entirely to the future. The judgment of the living and dead may also suggest
to us the just and unjust (53-55).

To the third article §§ 56-113 are devoted; it
is accordingly most elaborately elucidated. §§
56-63 treat of the Holy Ghost, who completes
the Trinity, and so is no part of creation, and
also of the Holy Church. This is the temple and
city of the Trinity. But it is here regarded as a
whole. That is, it includes the section which
exists in heaven and has never experienced a
fall—the angels who aid the pilgrim part (pars
peregrinans) being already united with it by
love (56). The Church in heaven is void of evil
and unchangeable. Augustine admits that he

[1] "Nihil aliud nisi similitudo mortis Christi; nihil autem
aliud mortem Christi crucifixi nisi remissionis peccati
similitudinem, ut quemadmodum in illo vera mors facta
est, sic in nobis vera remissio peccatorum."

[2] "Ita gestum est, ut his rebus non mystice tantum
dictis sed etiam gestis configuraretur vita Christiana
quæ hic geritur."

does not know whether there are degrees of rank among the angels, whether the stars belong to them, or what the truth is as to their bodily form (57-59). It is more important to determine when Satan invests himself in the form of an angel of light (60). We shall only know the state of the heavenly Church when we belong to it ourselves. The Church of this world, for which Christ died, we do know; for the angels he did not die; yet the result of his work also extends to them, in so far as enmity to them is at an end, and their number is once more complete. Thus by the one sacrifice the earthly host is again united with the heavenly, and the peace is restored that transcends all thought— not that of angels, but of men; but even angels, and men who have entered the state of felicity, will never comprehend the peace of God as God himself does (61-63).

Augustine now passes to the "remission of sins" (64-83): "by this stands the Church on earth (per hanc stat ecclesia quæ in terris est). So far as our sins are forgiven, "the angels are even now in harmony with us" (concordant nobiscum angeli etiam nunc). In addition to the "great indulgence," there is a continuous remission of sins, which even the most advanced of the righteous need, for they often descend to their own level and sin. Certainly the life of the saints may be free from transgressions, but not from sin (64). But even for grave offences there is forgiveness in the Church after due penance; and the important point is not the time of penance, but the anguish of the penitent. But since this emotion is concealed from our fellow-men, and cannot be inspected, the bishops have rightly instituted penitential seasons "that the Church may also be satisfied," the Church beyond whose pale there is no forgiveness; for it alone has received the pledge of the Holy Ghost (65). Evils remain in this world in spite of the *salutaria sacramenta,* that we may see that the future state is their goal. There are punitive evils; for sins last on, and are punished in this life or the next (66). We must certainly not fancy that faith by itself protects from future judgment ($\dot{\omega}_s$ $\delta\iota\dot{\alpha}$ $\pi\upsilon\rho\dot{o}_s$), it is rather only the faith that works in love (faith and works). By "wood and stubble" we are not to understand sins, but desires after earthly things lawful in themselves (67, 68). It is credible that a purifying fire exists for *believers even after death* (69)—sinners can only be saved by a corresponding penance combined with almsgiving. Almsgiving is now discussed in detail (69-77). At the Last Judgment the decision turns on it (Mat. XXV. 34 ff.). Of course we are at the same time to amend our lives; "God is to be propitiated for past sins by alms, not by any means to be bribed that we may always be allowed to commit sins with impunity." [1] God blots out sins "if due satisfaction is not neglected" (si satisfactio congrua non negligatur), without giving permission to sin (70). Daily

[1] "Per eleemosynas de peccatis præteritis est propitian-dus deus, non ad hoc emendus quodam modo, ut peccata semper liceat impune committere." Accordingly some Catholics must even then have looked on alms as conferring a license.

prayer furnishes satisfaction for small and light
daily sins (71).[1] The forgiveness, also, that we
bestow on others is a kind of alms. Speaking
generally, everything good we give to others,
advice, comfort, discipline, etc., is alms. By this
we besides help to gain forgiveness of our own
sins (72). But the highest stages of almsgiving
are forgiveness of sins and love of our enemies
(73).[2] Those virtues everyone must practise,
that he himself may be forgiven (74). But all
these alms fail to benefit us unless we amend
ourselves; that is, the alms we give to ourselves
are the most important. Of him alone who has
mercy on himself is the saying true: "Give alms
and all is right (pure) with you." We must love
ourselves with the love that God has bestowed
on us; this the Pharisees, who only gave outward alms, did not do, for they were the enemies
of their own souls (75-77). The divine judgment, however, can alone determine what sins
are light or grave. Many things permitted by the
apostles—e.g., matrimonial intercourse prompted
by desire—are yet sinful; many sins which we
consider wholly trifling (e.g., reviling), are
grave; and many—e.g., unchastity—which cus-
tom has brought us to look on lightly, are dread-
ful, even though Church discipline itself has
become lax in dealing with them (78-80). All
sin springs either from ignorance or weakness.

[1] "Delet omnino hæc oratio minima et quotidiana
peccata."
[2] Augustine here says with great truth that love of
our enemies is possible only to a small minority (the
perfect). But even those who do not attain it are heard if
they utter the fifth petition in faith.

The latter is the more serious; but divine grace alone aids us to overcome either (81). Unfortunately, from false weakness and shame, public penance is frequently withheld. Therefore God's mercy is not only necessary in the case of penitence, but also that men may resolve to show penitence. But he who disbelieves in and despises the forgiveness of sin in the Church commits the sin against the Holy Ghost (82, 83).

The resurrection of the body is dealt with in §§ 84-113. First, the resurrection of abortions and monstrosities is discussed (85-87); then the relation of the new body to its old material—every particle of which need not pass into the former; and further, the corporeal difference, the stainlessness and spirituality of bodies in the future state (88-91). We must not concern ourselves with the constitution of the bodies of the lost who also rise again, although we are here confronted by the great paradox that a corruptible body does not die nor an incorruptible feel pain.[1] (92). Those will have the mildest punishment who have only original, but not actual, sin. Damnation in general will be marked by degrees, depending in each case on the measure of sin (93). Augustine now comes to speak of predestination in detail (94-108): "no one is saved except by undeserved mercy, and no one is condemned except by a deserved judgment."[2] That is the theme. It will become manifest in eternal life *why* of two

[1] In hell "mors ipsa non moritur."
[2] "Nisi per indebitam misericordiam nemo liberatur et nisi per debitum judicium nemo damnatur."

children the one is accepted out of mercy, and the other rejected in accordance with justice. God's refusal of salvation is not unjust, though all might have been saved if he had willed; for nothing happens without his will or permission (95). Even in permitting evil his action is good, or the first article of the Symbol would no longer hold true (96). But if God's will cannot be frustrated by any choice of his creatures, how does the fact that all are not saved agree with the assurance that "he wills that all should be saved" (1 Tim. II. 4)? The usual answer, that men will not, is obviously false; for they cannot hinder God's will, as he can certainly turn even the bad into a good will. Accordingly, God does not will that all be saved, but he justly sentences sinners to death (Rom. IX.), that he who receives salvation may boast in the Lord. God is free in his election to grace; he would not have been to be blamed if he had redeemed no one after Adam's Fall; so neither is he to be blamed if in his mercy he redeems only a few, that none may boast of his own merits, but in the Lord. God's will is expressed in the case of the lost as much as in that of the saved ("in the very deed by which they opposed his will, his will regarding them was done").[1] So great are the works of the Lord that nothing that takes place against his will happens outside (præter) of it. A good son wishes his father to live, but God, whose will is good, decides that he should die. Again, a bad

---

[1] "Hoc ipso quod contra voluntatem fecerunt ejus, de ipsis facta est voluntas ejus."

son wishes his father to die, and God also wills this. The former wills what God does not; the latter what he does. Yet the former stands nearer God; for in the case of men it is the final intention that counts, while God accomplishes his good will even through the bad will of men. He is always just and always omnipotent (97-102). Therefore 1 Tim. II. 4 can only mean that God wills all *classes* of men to be saved, or that all those whom he resolves to save will be saved. In any case it is not to be imagined that he desires to save all, but is prevented (103).

Had God foreknown that Adam, in keeping with his constitution, would have retained forever the will to avoid sin, he would have preserved him in his original state of salvation. But he knew the opposite, and therefore shaped his own will to effect good through him who did evil. For man must have been so created originally as to be able to do good and evil. Afterwards he will be changed, and will no longer be able to will evil; "nor will he therefore be without free choice" (nec ideo libero carebit arbitrio); for free will still exists, even if a time comes when we cannot will evil, just as it even now exists, although we can never will our own damnation. Only the order of things had to be observed, first the "posse non," then the "non posse." But grace is always necessary, and would have been even if man had not sinned; for he could only have attained the "non posse" by the co-operation of grace. (Men can indeed starve voluntarily, but mere appetite will not keep them alive; they require food.) But since sin entered, grace is much greater, because the will had itself to be freed in order that it might co-operate with grace (104-106). Eternal life, though a reward of good works, is also a gift of grace, because our merits are God's gifts. God has made one vessel to honour and another to dishonour, that none should boast. The mediator who redeemed us required also to be God, "that the pride of man might be censured by the humility of God" (ut superbia humana per humilitatem dei argueretur), and that man might be shown how far he had departed from God, etc. (107, 108). After this long excursus, Augustine returns to § 93, and deals (109) with the intermediate state (in abditis receptaculis), and the mitigation obtained by departed souls through the Mass, and the alms of survivors in the Church; for there are many souls not good enough to be able to dispense with this provision, and not bad enough not to be benefited by it. "Wherefore here (on the earth) all merit is acquired by which anyone can be relieved or burdened after this life." [1] What the Church does for the dead (pro defunctis commendandis) is not inconsistent with Rom. XIV. 10; II. Cor. V. 10. For those who are wholly good it is a thanksgiving, for those not altogether bad an atonement, for those entirely wicked it is resultless, but gives comfort to the survivors; nay, while it makes remission complete (plena), it renders damnation more tolerable (110). After the Judgment there are only two states,

[1] Quocirca hic (in terra) omne meritum comparatur, quo possit post hanc vitam relevari quispiam vel gravari.

though there are different grades in them. We
must believe in the eternal duration of the pains
of hell, although we may perhaps suppose that
from time to time God lightens the punishment
of the lost, or permits some sort of mitigation.
"Death will continue without end, just as the
collective eternal life of all saints will continue"
(111-113).[1]

Following his programme, Augustine ought
now to have discussed in detail hope and love
(prayer); but he omits doing so, because he
has really touched on everything already. He
therefore confines himself to affirming that hope
applies solely to what we pray for in the Lord's
Prayer, that three petitions refer to eternal, four
to temporal, benefits, and that Matthew and
Luke do not really differ in their versions of the
Prayer (114-116). As regards love, he points out
that it is the greatest of all. It, and not faith and
hope, decides the measure of goodness possessed
by a man. Faith and hope can exist without
love, but they are useless. The faith that works
in love, i.e., the Holy Spirit by whom love is
infused into our hearts, is all-important; for
where love is wanting, fleshly lust reigns (117).
There are four human conditions: life among the
deepest shades of ignorance (altissimis igno-
rantiæ tenebris), under the law (which produces
knowledge and conscious sin), under grace or
good hope, and under peace (in the world
beyond). Such has also been the history of
God's people; but God has shown his grace even

---

[1] Manebit sine fine mors, sicut manebit communiter
omnium vita æterna sanctorum.

at the first and second stages (118), and thus
even now man is laid hold of sometimes at the
first, sometimes at the second, stage, all his sins
being forgiven in his regeneration (119), so
that death itself no longer harms him (120). All
divine commands aim at love, and no good, if
done from fear of punishment or any other
motive than love, is done as it ought. All precepts (mandata) and counsels (consilia) given
by God are comprised in the command to love
God and our neighbour, and they are only
rightly performed when they spring, at present
in faith, in the future in immediate knowledge,
from love. In the world of sight each will know
what he should love in the other. Even now
desire abates as love increases, until it reaches
the love that leads a man to give his life for
another. But how great will love be in the future
state, when there no longer exists any desire
to be overcome!

No one can mistake the popular Catholic
features of this system of religion. It is based
on the ancient Symbol. The doctrines of the
Trinity and the Two Natures are faithfully
avowed. The importance of the Catholic Church
is strictly guarded, and its relation to the heavenly Church, which is the proper object of
faith, is left as indefinite as the current view
required. Baptism is set in the foreground as
the "grand mystery of renovation," and is derived from Christ's death, in which the devil
has obtained his due. Faith is only regarded as
a preliminary condition; eternal life is only

imparted to *merits* which are products of grace and freedom. They consist of works of love, which are summed up in almsgiving. Almsgiving is freely treated; it constitutes penance. Within the Church forgiveness is to be had for all sins after baptism, if only a fitting satisfaction is furnished (satisfacere ecclesiæ; satisfactio congrua). There is a scale of sins, from crimes to quite trivial daily offences. For this reason, wicked and good men are graded; but even the best (sancti, perfecti) can only be sinless in the sense that they commit none but the lightest sins. The saints are the perfect ascetics; asceticism is the culmination of love; but all do not need to practise it; we must distinguish between commands and counsels. In the future state both felicity and perdition will also be graded. Departed souls, if at death they have only left trivial sins unatoned for by penance, will be benefited by the masses, alms, and prayers of survivors. They are placed in a purgatory that cleanses them in the form of a decreed punishment.[1] If here popular Catholic elements are already strengthened, and the way prepared for their future elaboration, that is equally true of the doctrines of the intermediate state, the temporary mitigation of the punishment of the lost, the help afforded by holy angels to the Church of the present world, the completion—by means of redeemed mortals—of the heavenly Church reduced in number through the Fall of the wicked angels, the virginity of Mary even

[1] The Enchiridion is not the only work in which Augustine has spoken of this *ignis purgatorius.*

in partu,[1] and the grace of Christ as being
greater than Adam's sin. This also applies to
the opinion that the ignorant adherence to a
false religion is worse than the knowing utter-
ance of a lie, and to many other doctrines de-
veloped by Augustine in other writings. Finally,
the conception of salvation that holds it to consist in "vision" and "fruition" is at the root of
and runs through everything. Yet the most
spiritual fact, the process of sanctification, is
attached to mysteriously operating forces.

But on the other hand, this system of religion
is new. The old Symbol—the Apostles interpreted by the Nicene—was supplemented by

[1] The growing Marian dogma (see Vol. IV., p. 314)
was thus strengthened rather than weakened by Augustine. He agreed entirely with Ambrose and Jerome
(against Jovinian). By a woman came death, by a
woman came life; Mary's faith conceived the Saviour.
Julian's remarkable objection to the doctrine of original
sin, that it made Mary to be subject to the devil (nascendi
conditione), Augustine met by saying (Op. imp. IV.
122): "ipsa conditio nascendi solvitur gratia renascendi."
We may not maintain it to be certain (see Schwane II.,
p. 691 f.) that Augustine thus implicitly taught Mary's
immaculate conception. On the other hand, he undoubtedly held her to be without active sin; see De nat. et gr.
36: "Excepta itaque s. virgine Maria, de qua propter
honorem domini nullam prorsus, cum de peccatis agitur,
haberi volo quæstionem; unde enim scimus, quid ei plus
gratiæ collatum fuerit ad vincendum omni ex parte
peccatum, quæ concipere et parere meruit, quem constat
nullum habuisse peccatum? hac ergo virgine excepta si
omnes illos sanctos et sanctas, cum hic viverent, con-
gregare possimus et interrogare, utrum essent sine peccato, quid fuisse responsuros putamus, utrum hoc quod
ista dicit an quod Johannes apostolus?" Gen. ad litt. X.
18-21. Augustine helped to give Mary a special position
between Christ and Christians, simply because he first
emphasised strongly the sinfulness of all men, even the
saints, and then *excepted Mary.* Mary's passive receptivity
in relation to grace is emphasised with the same words
as that of the man Jesus.

new material which could only be very loosely
combined with it, and which at the same time
modified the original elements. *In all three
articles the treatment of sin, forgiveness, and
perfecting in love is the main matter* (10-15; 25-
33; 41-52; 64-83). Everything is presented as a
spiritual process, to which the briefly discussed
old dogmatic material appears subordinated.
Therefore, also, the third article comes into the
foreground; a half of the whole book is devoted
to the few words contained in it. Even in the
outline, novelty is shown: religion is so much
a matter of the inner life that faith, hope, and
love are all-important (3-8). *No cosmology is
given in the first article;* indeed, physical teaching is expressly denied to form part of dogmatics (9, 16 f.). *Therefore any Logos doctrine
is also wanting.* The Trinity, taught by tradition
as dogma, is apprehended in the strictest unity;
it is the creator. It is really one person; the
"persons," as Augustine teaches us in other
writings, are *inner* phases (moments) in the
one God; they have no cosmological import.
Thus the whole Trinity also created the man
Christ in Mary's womb; the Holy Ghost is only
named because "spiritus" is also a term for
"God's gift" (donum dei). Everything in religion relates to God as *only* source of all *good,*
and to *sin;* the latter is distinguished from *error.*
Hereby a breach is made with ancient intel-
lectualism, though a trace of it remains in the
contention that errors are very small sins. Wher-
ever sin is thought of, so is free, predestinating
grace (gratia gratis data). The latter is con-

trasted with the sin inherited from Adam; it
first gives freedom to the enslaved will. The
exposition of the first article closes with the
reference to prevenient and subsequent mercy.
How different would have been the wording of
this article if Augustine had been able to give
an independent version!

The case is not different with the second
article. The actual contents of the Symbol are
only briefly touched on—the Second Advent is
merely mentioned without a single Chiliastic
observation. On the other hand, the following
points of view come to the front. On the one
side we have the *unity* of Christ's personality as
the man (homo) with whose soul the Word
united itself, *the predestinating grace,* that introduced this man into personal unity with the
Deity, although he possessed no merits (hence
the parallel with our regeneration); the close
connection of Christ's death with redemption
from the devil, atonement, and baptism (forgiveness of sins). But on the other side we find
*the view of Christ's appearance and history as
loftiness in humility, and as the pattern of the
Christian life.* Christ's significance as redeemer[1]
is quite as strongly expressed for Augustine in
this humility in splendour, and in his example
of a Christian life (see S. Bernard and S. Fran-
cis), as in his death. He fluctuates between
these two points of view. The Incarnation
wholly recedes, or is set in a light entirely un-

[1] Sin and original sin are again discussed in §§ 41-52,
but they are now looked at from the standpoint of their
removal through the baptism that emanates from Christ's
death.

familiar to the Greeks. Thus the second article has been completely changed.

The chief and novel point in the third article consists in the freedom and assurance with which Augustine teaches that the forgiveness of sins in the Church is inexhaustible. When we consider the attitude of the ancient Church, Augustine, and Luther, to the sins of baptised Christians, an external criticism might lead us to say that men grow more and more lax, and that the increasing prominence given to grace (the religious factor) was merely a means of evading the strict demands made by the gospel on morality—the Christian life. And this view is also correct, if we look at the great mass of those who followed those guides. But in their own case their new ideas were produced by a profounder consciousness of sin, and an absorption in the magnitude of divine grace as taught by Paul. Augustine stands midway between the ancient Church and Luther. The question of personal assurance of salvation had not yet come home to him; but the question: "How shall I get rid of my sins, and be filled with divine energy?" took the first place with him. Following the popular Catholic view, he looked to good works (alms, prayer, asceticism); but he conceived them to be the product of grace and the will subject to grace; further, he warned Christians against all external doing. As he set aside all ritualistic mysticism, so he was thoroughly aware that nothing was to be purchased by almsgiving pure and simple, but that the issue depended on an inner transformation, a

pure heart, and a new spirit. At the same time
he was sure that even after baptism the way of
forgiveness was ever open to the penitent, and
*that he committed the sin against the Holy
Ghost who did not believe in this remission of
sins in the Church.* That is an entirely new
interpretation of the Gospel saying. The concluding section of the Symbol (resurrectio car-
nis) is explained even more thoroughly than
the forgiveness of sins in its third treatment in
the third article. But after a short discussion of
the subject proper—the *doctrine of predestination*[1] and a view which as doctrine is likewise
virtually new, and takes the place of Origen's
theory of Apokatastasis—the main theme is the

---

[1] The doctrine of predestination—before Augustine al-
most unheard of in the Catholic Church—constituted the
power of his religious life, as Chiliasm did that of the
post-apostolic, and mysticism that of the Greek Church.
In Augustine, in addition to its Biblical and Neoplatonic
supports, the doctrine had indeed a strong religious root
—free grace (gratia gratis data). But the latter by itself
does not explain the importance which the doctrine had
gained in his case. As everything that lives and works in
nature is attached to something else, and is never found
in an *independent* state, so, too, there is no distilled
piety. On the contrary, so long as we men are men, precisely the most vital piety will be least isolated and free.
None but the dogmatist can construct such a religion.
But history teaches that all great religious personalities
have connected their saving faith inextricably with con-
victions which to the reflecting mind appear to be ir-
relevant additions. In the history of Christianity there
are the three named—Chiliasm, mysticism, and the
doctrine of predestination. It is in the bark formed by
these that faith has grown, just as it is not in the middle
of the stem, but at its circumference, where stem and
bark meet, that the sap of the plant flows. Strip the tree,
and it will wither! Therefore it is well-meant, but foolish,
to suppose that Augustine would have done better to
have given forth his teaching without the doctrine of
predestination.

supposition of an intermediate state, and of a cleansing of souls in it, to which the offerings and prayers of survivors can contribute.

Piety: *faith* and *love* instead of fear and hope. Theory of religion: something higher than aught we call doctrine, a new *life* in the power of love. The doctrine of Scripture: the substance—the gospel, faith, love and hope—God. The Trinity: the one living God. Christology: the one mediator, the man Jesus into union with whose soul the Deity entered, without that soul having deserved it. Redemption: death for the benefit of enemies and humility in greatness. The Sacraments: the Word side by side with the Symbols. Salvation (felicity): the *beata necessitas* of the *good. The good:* blessedness in *dependence on God.* History: *God works everything in accordance with His good pleasure.* With that compare the dogmatics of the Greeks![1] . . .

It has been said of Socrates that he brought philosophy down from heaven; we may maintain of Augustine that he did the same for dogmatics, by separating it from speculations about the finite and infinite, God the Logos and the creature, mortal and immortal, and connecting

[1] An excellent comparison between Origen and Augustine occurs in Bigg, The Christian Platonists, pp. 284-290. He has sharply emphasised the inconsistencies in Augustine's doctrine of the primitive state, original sin, and grace, but he has not overlooked the advance made by Augustine on Origen. If we evolve Augustine's doctrine from predestination, then Bigg is right when he says: "Augustine's system is in truth that of the Gnostics, the ancestors of the Manichees. For it makes no real difference whether our doom is stamped upon the nature given to us by our Creator, or fixed by an arbitrary decree."

it with questions as to moral good, freedom, sin, and blessedness. *Goodness became for him the point on which turned the consideration of blessings;* moral goodness (virtue) and the possession of salvation were not merely to occupy corresponding positions, but to coincide (ipsa virtus et praemium virtutis). If we may use a figure, we can say that Augustine formed into one the two centres of popular Catholic theology, the renewing power of redemption and the free effort to attain virtue; of the ellipse he made a circle—God, whose grace delivers the will and endows it with power to do what is good. In this is comprehended his significance in the history of the Christian religion.